ONE-POT
GLUTEN-FREE
cooking

ONE-POT
GLUTEN-FREE
cooking

Delicious Recipes with Easy Cleanup—**in 30 Minutes or Less!**

AMY RAINS
founder of *Wholesomelicious*

PAGE STREET
PUBLISHING CO.

PAGE STREET
PUBLISHING CO.

First published in 2018 by
Page Street Publishing Co.
27 Congress Street, Suite 105
Salem, MA 01970
www.pagestreetpublishing.com

Distributed by Macmillan, sales in Canada by The Canadian Manda Group.

22 21 20 19 18   1 2 3 4 5

ISBN-13: 978-1-62414-664-0
ISBN-10: 1-62414-664-3

Library of Congress Control Number: 2018952333

Cover and book design by Sara Pollard for Page Street Publishing Co.
Photography by Amy Rains
Cover photo by Sarah Fennel

Printed and bound in the United States

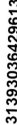

For Jeff, Addy and Luke: My three favorite people to cook for. Enjoying these recipes around our dining room table is my favorite time of the day!

CONTENTS

INTRODUCTION

For as long as I can remember, I have been looking forward to my next meal. Whether I was a little girl with a few coins in my hand at the baseball field concession stand or eating out at my favorite local authentic Mexican restaurant, meals have always been the most exciting time of day. Not much has changed!

My love for cooking started as soon as I turned sixteen and got my driver's license. My parents were busy raising three kids and, quite frankly, tired of cooking for all of us. I'm sure many of you can relate! My mom gave me a modest grocery budget and the keys to her car, and off I went. I continued to cook for myself throughout college. At the age of twenty-two, I was desperately trying to impress a certain thirty-year-old man with my cooking skills. Impressed he was—we were married eighteen months after the first meal I ever prepared for him. Fifteen years later, my husband continues to be my biggest fan and he loves testing each of my new recipes. We have traveled together to over thirty countries and even lived in Germany for four years. Many of the recipes I have developed were inspired by our travels; I was always searching for something special, unique and delicious to eat on our many adventures.

I've always been a foodie, but after completing a MS in Human Nutrition, I became a nutritionist too! I firmly believe the very best meals are made with simple and real ingredients. I have gradually transitioned to a gluten-free diet—by choice—because I feel my best when eating gluten free. This book is full of recipes that are naturally gluten free using nature's best vegetables, herbs and delicious spices.

My blog, wholesomelicious.com, has been my personal creative outlet to share my concoctions with others. The most popular recipes are those made with just one pan, in less than thirty minutes. As a super busy mom who spends most evenings at the ball fields (and yes, I am most definitely the loudest, er . . . most passionate mom there), I have made it my mission to create nutritious and delicious meals for my family. Easy, nutritious and kid-friendly recipes have enabled us to permanently avoid the drive-thru, and my most standout ones are in your very hands. My sincere hope is that this cookbook earns a permanent place in your kitchen, with dog-eared pages and sauces splattered across the recipes. Enjoy!

Note: The chapters are broken down by the pan or appliance needed. Learn more on page 176.

The SHEET PAN

A sheet pan meal has become my new favorite way to feed my family in a pinch! I love the clean and hands-off method that allows my oven to do all the work. Although this chapter contains breakfast, appetizers and even dessert, main dish recipes make up the bulk.

Sheet pan cooking produces flavorful browning and maximizes juiciness. I balance my meals with a protein, vegetable and a simple sauce or marinade. Most of these recipes are complete, while some may be best served over simple sides like rice, cauliflower rice, potatoes or a simple salad.

CASHEW CHICKEN AND VEGGIES

This cashew chicken will replace any desire to visit your local take-out Asian restaurant. The sauce is simple and so incredibly flavorful! It's sure to be gobbled up by family members of all ages. This much healthier variation of take-out, packed with different veggies and a delicious variety of textures, is also a cinch to make any night of the week. You know it's a winner-winner-chicken-dinner when the most difficult part of the dish is chopping the vegetables!

SERVES 4

For the Sauce

½ cup (120 ml) gluten-free tamari soy sauce or coconut aminos

⅓ cup (80 ml) apple cider vinegar

1 tbsp (15 ml) raw honey

2 tbsp (30 ml) orange juice

1 tbsp (15 ml) chili garlic sauce

1 tbsp (16 g) cashew butter (or any nut butter)

1 tbsp (12 g) coconut sugar or brown sugar

1 tsp chopped fresh ginger

1 tbsp (8 g) arrowroot starch

For the Chicken

1½ lb (680 g) boneless, skinless chicken breast, cut into 1-inch (2.5-cm) pieces

12 oz (340 g) broccoli florets, chopped

1 red bell pepper, diced

1 green bell pepper, diced

Rice or cauliflower rice, for serving

¾ cup (110 g) unsalted cashews, for garnish

2 tbsp (18 g) sesame seeds, for garnish

2 tbsp (18 g) diced green onion, for garnish, optional

Preheat the oven to 375ºF (190ºC) and arrange the oven rack in the center position. Lightly grease a large sheet pan with cooking spray.

For the sauce, whisk together the gluten-free soy sauce, apple cider vinegar, raw honey, orange juice, chili garlic sauce, cashew butter, coconut sugar, fresh ginger and arrowroot starch in a medium-size bowl. Reserve ⅓ cup (80 ml) of the sauce for serving.

Place the chicken, broccoli, red bell pepper and green bell pepper in a large bowl, and cover with the sauce. Mix, then spread the mixture evenly over the sheet pan. Transfer the pan to the oven.

Bake for 20 to 22 minutes, or until the chicken is done and the veggies are tender-crisp.

Remove the pan from the oven. Serve hot over rice or cauliflower rice with unsalted cashews, sesame seeds and green onions (if using), and add the reserved sauce.

CILANTRO LIME SHRIMP FAJITAS

Roasting shrimp in a sheet pan is the ultimate way to get the juiciest and most flavorful shrimp ever! I absolutely love how this dinner is baked in less than ten minutes—what can be better than that on a busy weeknight? These fajitas taste delicious wrapped in gluten-free tortillas, over a bowl of rice or on top of a salad. Oh, and the cilantro lime marinade will become your new obsession. Pinky promise!

SERVES 4

For the Marinade

½ cup (120 ml) avocado oil or olive oil

Juice of 1 lime, plus more to taste

1 tbsp (15 ml) red wine vinegar

½ cup (8 g) chopped fresh cilantro, divided

1 tsp cumin

1 tsp chili powder

½ tsp Kosher salt

For the Fajitas

1½ lb (680 g) raw shrimp, peeled and deveined with tails removed

1 red bell pepper, cut into strips

1 green bell pepper, cut into strips

1 small red onion, thinly sliced

Gluten-free tortillas, optional

Preheat the oven to 450°F (230°C) and arrange the oven rack in the center position. Line a large baking sheet with foil or lightly grease with a nonstick spray. Set aside.

Prepare a quick marinade for the shrimp. Whisk together (or blend in a food processor or blender) the oil, lime juice, red wine vinegar, ⅓ cup (5 g) of the cilantro, cumin, chili powder and salt. Pour the marinade over the shrimp while the oven heats up.

Line the red bell pepper, green bell pepper and red onion over the bottom of the sheet pan. Pour the shrimp with the marinade over the top; spread around the marinade to evenly coat the vegetables.

Place the pan in the oven and roast for 8 minutes, then broil for an additional 1 to 2 minutes or until the shrimp is cooked through.

Remove the pan from the oven, add the remaining cilantro over the top, place in tortillas (if using) and serve immediately!

GREEK CHICKEN

This super easy Greek Chicken is packed with tangy flavor, plenty of veggies and some fresh basil to make your taste buds sing! It is sure to become a weeknight staple. The ingredients can also combine for a warm Greek salad served over a bed of greens. Make this dish on the weekend to enjoy for lunches throughout the week!

SERVES 4

1½ lb (680 g) boneless, skinless chicken breast, diced into small pieces

2 tbsp (30 ml) olive oil or avocado oil

1 tbsp (15 ml) red wine vinegar

1 tbsp (15 ml) lemon juice

1 tsp Dijon mustard

1 tsp dried oregano

½ tsp Kosher salt, plus more to taste

1 red bell pepper, chopped

½ large red onion, chopped

1 cup (150 g) finely diced Yukon Gold potatoes

½ cup (75 g) marinated artichokes

½ cup (75 g) diced cherry tomatoes

⅓ cup (50 g) Kalamata olives

⅓ cup (50 g) crumbled feta cheese, optional

¼ cup (10 g) finely chopped fresh basil

Greens or rice, for serving

Ground black pepper, to taste

Preheat the oven to 375°F (190°C) and arrange the oven rack in the center position. Place the chicken in a large bowl or container.

In a separate bowl, whisk together the oil, red wine vinegar, lemon juice, Dijon, oregano and salt for a quick marinade. Pour it on top of the chicken.

Scatter the red bell pepper, red onion and potatoes across a large sheet pan. Then pour the chicken and marinade on top of the vegetables. Toss so that the chicken and vegetables are evenly coated with marinade and they remain in a single layer.

Place the chicken and veggies in the oven to bake for 15 minutes, then bump up the temperature to 425°F (218°C) to get everything extra toasty. Cook for another 10 to 12 minutes, or until the potatoes are softened and cooked through.

Remove the pan from the oven, add the artichokes, cherry tomatoes, Kalamata olives and feta cheese, if using. Top with fresh basil. Serve over a bed of greens or rice. Add salt and pepper to taste.

HERB AND MUSTARD PORK TENDERLOIN WITH SQUASH AND APPLES

The sheet pan method of cooking a pork tenderloin ensures it comes out perfect every time. The secret is the high heat, which allows this dish to cook beautifully in less than thirty minutes. This autumn-inspired dinner makes enough to feed a crowd or give you plenty of leftovers for throughout the week.

SERVES 6 TO 8

3 cups (420 g) butternut squash, peeled and chopped

2 apples, cored, peeled and chopped

½ large red onion, cut into slices

2 tbsp (30 ml) avocado oil or olive oil

2 cloves garlic, minced

1 tbsp (15 ml) lemon juice

1 tbsp (15 ml) real maple syrup

½ tsp sea salt

3 tsp (2 g) chopped fresh rosemary, divided

Pinch of ground black pepper

2 pork tenderloins (about 2½ lb [1.1 kg] total), trimmed of visible fat

1 tbsp (15 ml) Dijon mustard

3 tsp (6 g) Herbes de Provence

Heat the oven to 450°F (230°C) and arrange the rack in the center position.

Spray a large sheet pan with nonstick spray, then evenly spread the butternut squash, apples and red onion all over the pan. Whisk together the oil, garlic, lemon juice and maple syrup in a small bowl. Then drizzle or brush about 2 tablespoons (30 ml) of the mixture over the apples, squash and onion. Sprinkle with the sea salt, fresh rosemary and black pepper.

Pat the pork tenderloins with a paper towel, removing any excess moisture. Add the Dijon and Herbes de Provence to the remaining garlic/syrup mixture. Generously rub the mixture over both of the tenderloins, and place them on top of the squash, apples and onion.

Place the pan in the oven and cook for 15 minutes, then flip over the tenderloins. Cook for an additional 12 to 15 minutes (depending on thickness) and remove from the oven.

note   Golden Delicious apples work well in this recipe with their sweet, mellow flavor.

CHIMICHURRI STEAK AND POTATOES

Is there anything better than a steak and potato dinner? Oh yes, there is. Smother it in some chimichurri sauce and let it all bake on a sheet pan for the ultimate easy dinner! Chimichurri is a special sauce packed with fresh herbs, garlic, tangy lemon and vinegar and a little spice, if you're up for it. Although this may seem like a dinner for a special occasion, it's simple enough for weeknights.

SERVES 4 TO 6

1 cup (16 g) chopped fresh cilantro

1 cup (16 g) chopped fresh parsley

⅓ cup (50 g) chopped red onion

3 cloves garlic, minced

1 tsp chopped red hot chili pepper or crushed red pepper, optional

½ tsp sea salt, plus more to taste

¼ cup (60 ml) lemon juice

1 tsp lemon zest

¼ cup (60 ml) red wine vinegar

½ cup (120 ml) olive oil or avocado oil

2 lb (900 g) flank steak

3 large russet potatoes, cut into wedges (about 12–16 per potato)

Ground black pepper, to taste

Preheat the oven to 450°F (230°C) and arrange the rack in the center position.

In a food processor or blender, pulse together the cilantro, parsley, red onion, garlic, red hot chili pepper (if using), salt, lemon juice, lemon zest and red wine vinegar. While the motor is running, stream in the oil and continue to blend until smooth.

Place the flank steak in a dish or sealable bag, then pour ½ cup (120 ml) of the chimichurri sauce into the bag. Set aside.

Spread the potato wedges across the sheet pan, leaving room in the center for the flank steak. Gently toss with ¼ cup (60 ml) of chimichurri sauce. Sprinkle with salt and pepper.

Transfer the sheet pan to the oven and bake for 12 minutes. Remove the pan from the oven and flip the potatoes. Next, place the flank steak in the center of the pan.

Return the pan to the oven and bake for another 11 to 12 minutes. Turn on the broiler for another 2 minutes to get a nice sear on the steak.

Remove the pan from the oven and let it sit for 5 minutes. Slice the steak against the grain. Serve the steak and potatoes with the leftover chimichurri sauce.

THAI PEANUT COCONUT CHICKEN WITH PINEAPPLE AND VEGGIES

In some households, ranch dressing or ketchup are coveted condiments. In my household, peanut sauce is the ultimate boss! My kids call this dish "peanut butter chicken" and would happily eat it every day of the week. We all love the salty/sweet combo and the addition of pineapple. This dish is best served over rice or cauliflower rice.

SERVES 4

For the Peanut Sauce

¼ cup (60 ml) gluten-free tamari soy sauce or coconut aminos

3 tbsp (45 ml) apple cider vinegar

⅓ cup (85 g) peanut butter

¼ cup (60 ml) full-fat canned coconut milk

1 tbsp (15 ml) sesame oil

2 cloves garlic, crushed

1 tbsp (15 ml) raw honey

For the Chicken

1½ lb (680 g) chicken breast tenders

3 cups (270 g) broccoli florets or broccolini

1 red bell pepper, diced

2 cups (300 g) diced pineapple

1 tbsp (15 ml) olive oil or avocado oil

½ cup (75 g) chopped peanuts

2 tbsp (15 g) unsweetened shredded coconut

¼ cup (4 g) chopped fresh cilantro, optional

3 tbsp (18 g) chopped green onion, optional

Rice or cauliflower rice, for serving

Preheat the oven to 375°F (190°C) and arrange the oven rack in the center position.

In a food processor or blender, make the peanut sauce. Add the tamari soy sauce, apple cider vinegar, peanut butter, coconut milk, sesame oil, garlic and honey. Pulse until smooth. Reserve about ⅓ cup (80 ml) of the sauce for the finished dish.

Brush all sides of the chicken tenders with the sauce and arrange them in the center of the sheet pan. Place the broccoli, red bell pepper and pineapple around the chicken. Brush the vegetables and pineapple with oil, then the peanut sauce.

Bake for 18 to 20 minutes or until the chicken is cooked through. Top the chicken with peanuts and coconut. Turn on the broiler and place the pan back into the oven for an additional minute to get the chicken and veggies extra toasty.

Garnish with cilantro and green onion, if using. Serve over rice or cauliflower rice.

Feel free to swap out the peanut butter and peanuts with your nut butter of choice for any dietary restrictions or allergies.

MOROCCAN-SPICED SALMON WITH LEMON MINT YOGURT SAUCE

This dish has it all: flavor, beauty and ease. Isn't that what every weeknight dinner should have? I think so. The Moroccan rub is a perfect complement to the salmon and veggies and combines nicely with the lemon mint yogurt sauce. The best part about cooking salmon in a sheet pan is the quick cook time of less than 15 minutes. The carrots and green beans also roast very well at this temp and cook time, with a slight crunch and al dente texture!

SERVES 4

4 (5–6-oz [142–170-g]) skinless salmon fillets, about 1 inch (2.5 cm) thick

1 tsp cumin

1 tsp smoked paprika

½ tsp cinnamon

½ tsp coriander

¼ tsp cayenne pepper

¼ tsp ground black pepper

¼ tsp Kosher salt, plus more to taste

Pinch of ground cloves

8 oz (230 g) fresh green beans, trimmed

12 oz (340 g) sliced petite carrots (see note)

3 tbsp (45 ml) olive oil or avocado oil, divided

2 tbsp (30 ml) fresh lemon juice, divided

½ cup (100 g) plain Greek yogurt

½ tsp lemon zest

2 cloves garlic, minced

2 tbsp (30 g) chopped fresh mint

Fresh parsley, for garnish, optional

Preheat the oven to 425°F (218°C) and arrange the oven rack in the center position. Remove the salmon from your fridge and let it sit for at least 10 minutes, then pat dry with a paper towel. Line a large baking sheet with foil or parchment paper and set aside.

In a small bowl, make your spice rub. Mix together the cumin, paprika, cinnamon, coriander, cayenne pepper, black pepper, salt and cloves.

Place the green beans and carrots on the sheet pan. Toss with 1 to 2 tablespoons (15 to 30 ml) of oil and 2 teaspoons (4 g) of the spice rub, ensuring the veggies are evenly coated. Arrange the vegetables so they are lined up along the outside perimeter of the pan, leaving room in the middle for the salmon.

Place the salmon on the sheet pan. Brush with 1 tablespoon (15 ml) of oil, then gently rub the remaining spice rub all over the salmon fillets. Sprinkle with 1 tablespoon (15 ml) of lemon juice.

Bake for 8 to 12 minutes, depending on the thickness of the salmon. For a 1-inch (2.5-cm) piece of salmon, cook for approximately 8 minutes for medium rare, 10 minutes for medium or up to 12 minutes for medium-well.

While the salmon is baking, make the yogurt sauce. Whisk together the yogurt, remaining lemon juice, lemon zest, garlic, mint and salt to taste.

Remove the salmon from the oven and serve immediately with the sauce. Garnish with parsley (if using) and add salt to taste.

note: You can use any type of carrot—I used colored petite carrots from Trader Joe's—just slice them thinly so they cook evenly with the salmon.

ROSEMARY BALSAMIC CHICKEN WITH ASPARAGUS AND MUSHROOMS

The rosemary balsamic sauce in this dish is one of my all-time favorite marinades. I've been using it for years for grilling chicken and knew it would work well for an easy weeknight sheet pan meal. The flavor combination is perfect for mushrooms and asparagus, and I love the way it roasts deliciously on a sheet pan with the chicken. Serve with potatoes or rice for a complete meal, or even over a bed of greens for a roasted chicken and vegetable salad.

SERVES 4

⅓ cup (80 ml) balsamic vinegar

2½ tbsp (37 ml) olive oil or avocado oil

1 tbsp (15 ml) gluten-free tamari soy sauce or coconut aminos

2 tsp (8 g) coconut sugar

2 tbsp (8 g) finely chopped fresh rosemary

2 large cloves garlic, minced

1½ lb (680 g) boneless, skinless chicken breast, cut into bite-size pieces

1 lb (450 g) asparagus, cut into 3-inch (7.5-cm) pieces

10 oz (286 g) sliced mushrooms

Kosher salt, to taste

Preheat the oven to 375°F (190°C) and arrange the oven rack in the center position.

In a food processor or blender, combine the balsamic vinegar, oil, tamari soy sauce, coconut sugar, rosemary and garlic. Pulse until the ingredients are well combined, about 15 seconds.

In an airtight container or large sealable bag, combine the chicken, asparagus, mushrooms and marinade. Shake until all the ingredients are well covered in the marinade. You can marinate for up to 8 hours or proceed to bake.

Spread the mixture over your sheet pan. Bake for 15 minutes at 375°F (190°C), then bump up the temperature to 425°F (218°C) for the last 7 to 10 minutes.

Remove from the oven, salt to taste and serve hot.

CRISPY HONEY TURMERIC CHICKEN BUTTERNUT SQUASH

Glazed skin-on chicken thigh   sheet pan meals! The idea of a honey and turmeric chicken was inspired by my favorite drink, a golden latte. Turns out, this flavor medley also works well in savory dishes! The addition of butternut squash completes the meal with its earthy and subtly sweet flavor.

SERVES 4 TO 6

⅓ cup (80 ml) avocado oil or olive oil, divided

3 large cloves garlic, minced

3 tbsp (45 ml) fresh lemon juice

1 tbsp (15 g) ground turmeric

1 tsp cumin

1 tsp sea salt

1 tbsp (15 ml) honey

4 large bone-in, skin-on chicken thighs

2 cups (300 g) diced butternut squash, cut into small pieces less than ½ inch (1.3 cm)

Preheat the oven to 425°F (218°C) and arrange the oven rack in the top third of the oven. Coat a large baking sheet with 1 tablespoon (15 ml) of oil, and let it sit in the oven while it heats.

In a small bowl, whisk together the remaining oil with the garlic, lemon juice, turmeric, cumin, sea salt and honey. Place the chicken and butternut squash in a container or sealable bag with the glaze mixture, reserving 2 tablespoons (30 ml) of the glaze in the small bowl for later use. Evenly coat the chicken and squash.

Remove the heated sheet pan from the oven and spread out the chicken (skin side up) and butternut squash.

Roast the chicken and butternut squash for 15 minutes, then bump up the temperature to 450°F (232°C). Roast for another 10 to 12 minutes, or until the chicken skin is golden and crispy.

Remove from the oven and brush the remaining glaze over the chicken. Serve hot.

AVOCADO SUN-DRIED TOMATO TUNA CAKES

These tuna cakes are a twist on the classic crab cake: crisp and browned on the outside, soft and flavorful on the inside. Easy, packed with protein and omega-3s, budget-friendly and a perfect recipe to make ahead to enjoy as lunch throughout the week! Serve over a bed of greens with Avocado Cilantro Sauce (page 173), or in a lettuce burger topped with sliced avocado, tomatoes and onion.

SERVES 6

1 large ripe avocado

2 tbsp (20 g) diced marinated sun-dried tomatoes, drained

2 tbsp (20 g) diced red onion

2 (5-oz [142-g]) cans albacore tuna, drained

¼ cup (22 g) gluten-free rolled oats

3 tbsp (30 g) finely chopped pecans

2 tbsp (30 ml) fresh lemon juice

1 tsp Dijon mustard

1 tsp sea salt

1 tsp cumin

½ tsp garlic powder

1 egg, whisked

2 tbsp (5 g) chopped fresh basil

Preheat the oven to 400°F (204°C) and arrange the oven rack in the top third of your oven. Grease a large baking sheet with cooking spray and set aside.

In a large bowl, mash the avocado. Stir in the sun-dried tomatoes, red onion, tuna, oats, pecans, lemon juice, mustard, salt, cumin, garlic powder, egg and basil. Mix until well combined; the mixture will be chunky.

Form 6 patties and arrange them on your baking sheet.

Bake for 10 minutes, then bump the temperature to 425°F (218°C) and flip each patty over. Bake for another 8 to 10 minutes or until golden and crispy.

Remove the tuna cakes from the oven and let them sit for 2 to 3 minutes before removing from the pan.

note   Not all canned tuna is created equal. Certain canned tuna can be very high in mercury, and also caught in unethical ways. I've found that Wild Planet, Trader Joe's or even Starkist pouches are the best options for this recipe.

PESTO-STUFFED PORTOBELLO CAPS

Hearty and meaty, these portobello mushroom caps make a perfect bed for some fresh pesto. The portobellos can easily suffice for a Meatless Monday main course over a bed of greens or served as a side dish or appetizer alongside your favorite meat.

SERVES 6 TO 8

8 large portobello mushroom caps (see note)

2 tbsp (30 ml) olive oil or avocado oil

Sea salt and ground black pepper, to taste

1 cup (240 ml) high-quality pesto (see recipe for Basil Pesto on page 166)

¼ cup (25 g) freshly grated Parmesan, for serving

Preheat the oven to 400ºF (204ºC) and arrange your oven rack in the center position. Line a large sheet pan with foil, and lightly grease with cooking spray.

Gently scoop out the black gills of your portobello caps and discard. Brush oil inside the caps and sprinkle with some sea salt and black pepper. Arrange the mushrooms gill side down on the prepared baking sheet. Transfer to the oven and roast until tender, about 10 to 12 minutes.

Remove the pan from the oven, increase the temperature to 450ºF (232ºC) and flip the mushrooms over so they are gill side up. Spoon 1 to 2 tablespoons (15 to 30 ml) of pesto inside each mushroom cap. Return to the oven and bake for an additional 10 to 15 minutes, or until the mushrooms are nicely roasted and the pesto is bubbly.

Sprinkle with Parmesan cheese to serve.

note   Not to worry if your mushrooms don't have much of a "cup" shape; you can still get that delicious pesto taste around the edges of the portobellos.

SHRIMP POLENTA BITES
WITH FRESH HERBS AND TOMATOES

Call all of your best friends and get your outdoor space ready to party! These Shrimp Polenta Bites are the best kind of entertaining appetizer: gorgeous, refreshing, tasty and sure to become a favorite among your guests! You'll love the brilliant textures and flavors, and you'll find yourself wanting to make them often for an easy lunch or summertime dinner.

SERVES 6 TO 8

For the Bites

16-oz (454-g) tube pre-cooked polenta

12 oz (340 g) raw jumbo shrimp, peeled and deveined (see note)

For the Topping

1 cup (150 g) diced tomatoes

⅓ cup (50 g) diced cucumber

¼ cup (40 g) diced scallions (green and white parts)

2 tbsp (20 g) chopped fresh mint

1 tbsp (10 g) chopped fresh parsley

3 tbsp (45 ml) fresh lemon juice

Sea salt and ground black pepper, to taste

Preheat the oven to 400°F (204°C) and arrange your oven rack in the center position. Lightly grease a large sheet pan.

Slice your polenta tube into rounds, a little less than ½ inch (1 cm) thick. Arrange them on your sheet pan. Bake in the oven for 12 minutes.

Remove the polenta from the oven and place a piece of shrimp on each round. Return to the oven and bake for an additional 6 to 8 minutes, or until the shrimp is cooked through.

While the shrimp is in the oven, make the topping. Mix together the tomatoes, cucumber, scallions, mint, parsley and lemon juice. Sprinkle with sea salt to taste.

Remove the polenta bites from the oven. Spoon approximately 1 tablespoon (15 g) of topping on each bite. Sprinkle with additional salt and pepper if needed. Serve hot or at room temperature.

note   To save time, you can also buy pre-cooked shrimp. Bake the polenta for 15 to 18 minutes. Skip the third step, and instead, mix together the tomato topping with the shrimp.

LEMON BASIL PORK CHOPS AND ASPARAGUS

Thin-cut, boneless pork chops are actually a fantastic idea for an easy weeknight meal! They cook up in no time on a sheet pan and roast perfectly alongside some asparagus and tomatoes. The lemon basil sauce is similar to a pesto, but without the Parmesan. This easy dinner is an ode to my daughter, the pork chop and pesto lover!

SERVES 4 TO 6

⅓ cup (80 ml) olive oil or avocado oil

½ cup (8 g) fresh basil

Juice of 1 lemon

1 tsp lemon zest

½ tsp sea salt, plus more to taste

¼ tsp ground black pepper, plus more to taste

4–6 boneless pork chops (about ½ inch [13 mm] thick)

10 oz (283 g) asparagus spears, cut into 1–2-inch (2.5–5-cm) pieces

1 cup (150 g) cherry tomatoes

Preheat the oven to 425°F (218°C) and arrange the oven rack in the center position. Lightly grease a large sheet pan and set aside.

Using a blender or a food processor, pulse the oil, basil, lemon juice, lemon zest, salt and pepper. Place the sauce in a bowl or a sealable bag and coat the pork chops.

Spread the pork chops, asparagus and tomatoes across the sheet pan. Use any leftover sauce to coat the asparagus and tomatoes.

Transfer the pan to the oven. Bake until the pork chops are just cooked through, but still a bit pink on the inside, about 15 to 18 minutes.

Remove from the oven and serve hot. Season with salt and pepper to taste.

POTATO BREAKFAST NACHOS

My favorite junk food in the entire world is nachos; I've loved them since I was a little kid. Combining my love of nachos with my favorite breakfast combo of eggs and potatoes is pure gold! Thinly sliced potatoes serve as "chips" and taste absolutely delicious with a runny egg, chopped bacon, avocado and salsa. This simple meal can be a huge hit on weekends, or it makes an easy weeknight dinner. Breakfast for dinner, aka "brinner," is always welcome in my house!

SERVES 2

4 small Yukon Gold potatoes, thinly sliced

1 tbsp (15 ml) olive oil or avocado oil

½ tsp chili salt or season salt, plus more to taste

4 slices of bacon, chopped into small pieces

4 eggs

1 avocado, sliced

½ red onion, sliced

⅓ cup (50 g) chopped cherry tomatoes

2 tbsp (2 g) chopped fresh cilantro

⅓ cup (85 g) salsa, optional

Preheat the oven to 425°F (218°C) and arrange the oven rack in the center position. Lightly grease a sheet pan.

Arrange the potatoes in a single layer across the pan. Lightly brush with oil and sprinkle the salt across the potatoes evenly. Top the layer of potatoes with the chopped bacon. Place in the oven and bake for 12 to 15 minutes, or until the potato edges are browned and the bacon is crispy.

Remove the pan from the oven. Rearrange the potatoes in the pan so that you create four wells or spaces to add the eggs. Crack an egg in each space, ensuring the potatoes surround the eggs.

Bake for an additional 3 to 5 minutes, or until the egg whites are set and cooked to your desired doneness. Remove from the oven.

Using a spatula, remove the egg, potato and bacon mixture onto a plate to serve. Top with the avocado, onion, tomatoes, cilantro, more salt to taste and salsa, if using.

HONEY BUFFALO CHICKEN WINGS

Gather your football-loving friends for the next game and impress them with these delicious bites! A slightly sweetened twist to the typical buffalo wings baked to a crispy perfection, these make a perfect appetizer or even a main course dinner dish. Serve with your favorite dipping sauce, or try my Avocado Cilantro Sauce (page 173).

SERVES 6 TO 8

2½ lb (1.1 kg) chicken wings

1 tbsp (10 g) tapioca starch

1 tsp garlic powder

1 tsp onion powder

Pinch of Kosher salt

1 tbsp (15 ml) olive oil or avocado oil

½ cup (120 ml) buffalo wing sauce

1 tbsp (15 ml) raw honey

2 tbsp (10 g) diced green onion, for serving, optional

Preheat the oven to 425°F (218°C) and arrange the oven rack in the upper third of your oven. Lightly grease the sheet pan with cooking spray.

Using paper towels, remove any moisture from the chicken wings and set them aside.

In a small bowl, mix together the tapioca starch, garlic powder, onion powder and salt. Toss the chicken wings with the mixture and oil in a large bowl or container, evenly coating the wings. Spread out the wings on the sheet pan.

Bake for 15 minutes. Increase the temperature to 450°F (232°C) and flip the wings over. Cook for an additional 10 to 12 minutes or until crispy.

While the wings are baking, whisk together the buffalo wing sauce and honey.

Remove the wings from the oven and coat with the sauce. Serve hot with additional dipping sauce such as ranch or Avocado Cilantro Sauce (page 173). Garnish with green onion, if desired.

ROASTED CAULIFLOWER STEAKS

Cauliflower has become one of the most popular vegetables in recent years thanks to us gluten-free eaters! Admittedly, it's one of my least favorite vegetables raw, but when it's roasted, TOTAL GAME CHANGER. Cauliflower steaks are super fun as a side dish, topping on a salad or even beneath a tasty piece of protein. This recipe comes together with just a few simple ingredients but is certainly not lacking in the flavor department. You can fancy these up with my easy Basil Pesto (page 166) or Avocado Cilantro Sauce (page 173). Or just enjoy them as they are—I promise you'll love them!

SERVES 4 TO 6

2 large heads of cauliflower

¼ cup (60 ml) olive oil or avocado oil

4 cloves garlic, minced

Sea salt, to taste

Fresh ground black pepper, to taste

Juice of 1 lemon

Fresh parsley, for garnish, optional

Preheat the oven to 425ºF (218ºC) and arrange the oven rack in the top third of your oven. Remove the cauliflower stems, and place the cauliflower cut side down on a cutting board. Cut into ½-inch (1.3-cm) thick slices. Arrange the cauliflower on a baking sheet in one single layer.

In a small bowl, mix the oil and the garlic. Generously brush or spoon the oil/garlic mixture over each cauliflower steak. Season with salt and pepper.

Place your baking sheet in the oven on the middle rack. Bake for 20 to 25 minutes, flipping the cauliflower over after 10 minutes, until they have a nice golden-brown look, then remove them from the oven.

Top each steak with lemon juice, salt and pepper to taste and parsley, if using.

LAVENDER LEMON SHORTBREAD COOKIES

These delectable cookies have the most perfect texture—thick, chewy, buttery and just downright delicious! I'm a huge fan of lavender in my lattes or sweet treats and these cookies do it for me every time! They pair well with a cuppa tea or coffee and are just what you need for an afternoon pick-me-up.

YIELDS 1 DOZEN COOKIES

2¼ cups (245 g) blanched almond flour

¼ cup (30 g) coconut flour

1 tbsp (8 g) dried lavender buds

½ tsp baking soda

½ tsp sea salt

5 tbsp (75 g) unsalted grass-fed butter, softened or slightly melted

4 tbsp (60 ml) raw honey

2 tsp (10 g) lemon zest

1 tsp lemon extract

Preheat the oven to 350°F (177°C) and arrange the oven rack in the center position.

In a large bowl, mix together the almond flour, coconut flour, lavender buds, baking soda and sea salt.

In another bowl, beat the butter, honey, lemon zest and lemon extract. Fold the dry ingredients into the wet ingredients, continuing to mix until no dry flour pockets remain.

Using a spoon or small cookie scoop, spoon 1½- to 2-inch (4- to 5-cm) balls of the cookie dough onto a cookie sheet, leaving about 2 inches (5 cm) between the cookies. Gently flatten each cookie with the back of a spoon.

Place in the oven and bake for approximately 12 minutes. The edges should be lightly golden and the top should be firm, but the cookies will still be soft on the inside. Let the cookies cool for 10 minutes on your cookie sheet, and then remove from the pan.

HEALTHY OATMEAL RAISIN COOKIES

These are the cookies I bake when I want to feel like Mom of the Year. They are packed with protein and low in sugar, but still taste like the real deal. Delicious and soft with a buttery texture, they are so addicting! These cookies make a great school snack, lunchbox treat or even a grab-and-go breakfast. I also love that they bake in less than 10 minutes and without a mixer. Bonus: They're also easy enough for my ten-year-old to make without much supervision!

YIELDS 1 DOZEN COOKIES

1 cup (120 g) almond flour

1 cup (90 g) gluten-free rolled oats

⅓ cup (65 g) coconut sugar

2 tsp (5 g) cinnamon

½ tsp baking soda

¼ tsp sea salt

1 large egg, whisked

¼ cup (60 ml) coconut oil, melted

2 tbsp (30 g) almond butter

1 tsp vanilla extract

½ cup (75 g) raisins

Preheat the oven to 350°F (177°C) and arrange the oven rack in the center position. Line a large baking sheet with parchment paper or lightly grease with a nonstick spray. Set aside.

In a large mixing bowl, combine the almond flour, rolled oats, coconut sugar, cinnamon, baking soda and sea salt.

Add the egg, coconut oil, almond butter and vanilla. Continue to stir with a wooden spoon until no dry pockets remain. Fold in the raisins.

Using a cookie scoop or large spoon, scoop out the dough and roll it into a ball, using your hands if necessary. Place the dough on the cookie sheet about 2 inches (5 cm) apart, gently flattening the cookies with the back of a spoon.

Bake for 8 to 10 minutes, or until the top is slightly firm and lightly browned. Remove the cookies from the oven and let them cool on the pan completely.

Store the cookies in an airtight container for up to 1 week, or place in the freezer.

The
SKILLET

No kitchen is complete without a heavy and reliable skillet! One of the most durable kitchen tools that is often passed down from generation to generation is a cast-iron skillet. I love a cast-iron or ceramic skillet for its ability to hold heat and allow for a seamless transition from the stovetop to the oven.

Some of the recipes in this section will start with a sizzle on the stovetop and will finish off in the oven for a perfectly cooked and seasoned meal!

WARM BRUSSELS SPROUTS SALAD WITH AVOCADO AND BACON

"Best side dish ever!" says every person I have made this recipe for. The ingredient list speaks for itself, but if you happen to know a Brussels sprouts skeptic, you can easily win them over with this dish! It has become a staple in our home around the holidays, and something I love to whip up for a Sunday dinner. Don't limit this to a side dish; it can easily satisfy a hungry belly for dinner!

SERVES 4 TO 6

4 strips thick-cut bacon

½ red onion, thinly sliced

3 tbsp (45 ml) olive oil or avocado oil, divided

1 lb (450 g) Brussels sprouts, trimmed and halved

½ cup (120 ml) chicken broth

1 large avocado, cut into chunks

½ cup (75 g) diced pecans

Kosher salt and ground black pepper, to taste

2 tbsp (30 ml) red wine vinegar

1 tbsp (15 ml) honey

In a large cast-iron skillet or pan, cook the bacon over medium heat, until nice and crispy, about 6 to 8 minutes. Set aside the bacon, leave the pan hot and the bacon fat inside the pan. Once the bacon is cooled, crumble and set aside.

Add the onion to the bacon fat and cook until fragrant, for about 5 minutes. Set aside the onion and keep the pan hot.

Add 1 tablespoon (15 ml) of the oil to the pan, then add the Brussels sprouts. Cook the sprouts over medium-high heat for a few minutes, until they begin to brown. Add the chicken broth. Cook the Brussels sprouts for another 4 to 6 minutes or so, or until the broth has been reduced.

Transfer the Brussels sprouts to a serving dish, add in the onion, crumbled bacon, avocado and pecans. Season with salt and pepper.

In a small bowl, whisk together the remaining oil, red wine vinegar and honey and drizzle over the top of the salad. Serve warm. Season with additional salt and pepper if needed.

note: I will sometimes swap out the red wine vinegar for balsamic, or use almonds in place of pecans. You can't go wrong with either of these options.

LOADED BEEF TACO AND VEGGIE SKILLET

I grew up a Mexican food lover, and tacos were a regular meal every week. I carry on that tradition with my own kids, and Taco Tuesday is still my favorite night of the week! I always vary the way we do tacos each week, and this one is a personal favorite because of all the veggies. You will finish off this recipe in the oven to melt the cheese on top, but you can replace the cheese with a dairy-free option by substituting my Avocado Cilantro Sauce (page 173). This taco recipe is delicious alone, served over some greens for a taco salad or over a bed of rice. Don't be shy with those toppings—they are the best part!

SERVES 6

2 tbsp (30 ml) avocado oil or olive oil

1 small white onion, diced

1 medium sweet potato, peeled and diced into small pieces

1 green bell pepper, diced

1 lb (450 g) grass-fed ground beef

1 small zucchini, diced

2 tsp (5 g) cumin

2 tsp (5 g) smoked paprika

1 tsp chipotle chili powder

1 tsp chili powder

½ tsp Kosher salt

1 (14-oz [397-g]) can diced tomatoes

1 (4-oz [113-g]) can diced green chilis

1 tbsp (15 ml) apple cider vinegar

½ cup (60 g) shredded cheddar or pepper jack cheese, optional

¼ cup (10 g) chopped fresh cilantro, for garnish, optional

1 avocado, diced, for garnish, optional

Preheat the oven to 450°F (232°C) and arrange the oven rack in the top position. Heat a large cast-iron or ovenproof skillet to medium-high heat. Coat the bottom of your pan with oil.

Place the onion, sweet potato and green bell pepper in the pan. Sauté for 4 to 5 minutes, or until the veggies are fragrant and softened. Reduce the heat to medium and add in the ground beef and zucchini. Continue to cook until the ground beef is no longer pink, around 5 to 6 minutes. Drain any extra fat from the pan and bring it back to the heat.

Add the cumin, paprika, chipotle powder, chili powder and salt to the veggie/beef mixture. Mix until the veggies and beef are well coated, then add the tomatoes, chilis and apple cider vinegar. Continue to stir and simmer for another 5 minutes.

Sprinkle cheese on top of the mixture, if using. Place the skillet in the oven for 3 to 4 minutes, or until the cheese is bubbly. Remove the skillet from the oven and serve hot! Garnish with cilantro and avocado, if using.

PECAN-CRUSTED CHICKEN PICCATA

Am I allowed to have a favorite recipe "child" in this chapter? If so, I am totally admitting to this one. The pecans crust the chicken perfectly, adding a super yummy crunchy texture. And the lemon caper sauce with white wine? Ridiculously delicious. I make this dish often for dinner, but still not nearly enough. This is a meal that I gladly make to impress out-of-town visitors, but also one that the whole family happily devours on a busy weeknight.

SERVES 6

1 cup (150 g) chopped pecans

½ tsp Kosher salt

½ tsp lemon pepper

3 tbsp (45 ml) olive oil or avocado oil, divided

4 chicken breast cutlets, about ½ inch (1.3 cm) thick

2 cloves garlic, minced

1 lemon, juiced (about ¼ cup [60 ml])

1 cup (240 ml) white wine (or chicken broth)

2 tbsp (20 g) capers, drained

2 tsp (8 g) arrowroot starch, plus 2 tsp (10 ml) water

1 lemon, sliced, for garnish

2 tbsp (5 g) chopped fresh parsley, for garnish, optional

Zoodles, rice, cauliflower rice, potatoes or greens, for serving

Heat a large skillet over medium heat.

While the skillet is heating up, pulse the pecans, salt and lemon pepper in a food processor or blender for about 5 to 10 seconds until it resembles a coarse texture. Do not overpulse.

Place the pecan mixture into a shallow bowl near the stovetop. Add 2 tablespoons (30 ml) of oil to the skillet. Dredge each chicken cutlet in the pecan mixture, covering all sides evenly, then place in the hot skillet. Cook for approximately 5 to 6 minutes on each side. The chicken may still be a little pink (depending on thickness), but can still be set aside as it will be returned to the skillet to continue to cook in a few minutes.

Add the remaining tablespoon (15 ml) of oil to the hot skillet. Sauté the minced garlic for about 1 minute, and scrape around the bottom of the pan to pick up any loose pecans. Add in the lemon juice, white wine and capers. Increase the heat to medium-high and let the sauce come to a bubbly mixture, about 2 to 3 minutes. Mix together the arrowroot starch and water, and pour it into the lemon/caper sauce. Reduce the heat to low, continuing to stir.

As the sauce begins to thicken, add the chicken back to the pan. Simmer for another 3 to 4 minutes, or until the chicken is cooked through.

Serve hot, and spoon plenty of sauce over the chicken. Garnish with lemon slices and parsley, if using. Serve with zoodles, rice, cauliflower rice, potatoes or on top of a bed of greens.

SKILLET CHICKEN RATATOUILLE

Let's take the classic French summer dish and add some protein for a complete and healthy weeknight meal! Cooked vegetables are my favorite thing to eat, so this recipe is one I frequently make when spring and summer veggies are at their best. Visit your local farmers' market or spend a few minutes in your garden picking the season's best vegetables, then let your skillet do all the work.

SERVES 4

Kosher salt and ground black pepper

1 lb (450 g) boneless, skinless chicken breast, cut into chunks

1 tbsp (15 ml) olive oil or avocado oil

1 small sweet onion, diced

2 cloves garlic, minced

1 small zucchini, diced

1 yellow squash, diced

1 red bell pepper, diced

1 orange bell pepper, diced

1 cup (150 g) diced eggplant

1 cup (150 g) halved cherry tomatoes

2 tsp (5 g) Italian seasoning

1 tsp Kosher salt, plus more to taste

1 tbsp (16 g) tomato paste

1 tbsp (15 ml) red wine vinegar

⅓ cup (5 g) fresh basil, chopped, for garnish

1 tbsp (3 g) fresh thyme, for garnish

Heat your skillet to medium heat. Salt and pepper the chicken. Once the skillet is hot, coat the pan with oil and add the chicken. Cook for 3 to 4 minutes, continuing to stir so that all sides of the chicken are starting to brown.

Add the onion and garlic to the skillet and cook for an additional 3 minutes. Stir in the zucchini, yellow squash, red bell pepper, orange bell pepper, eggplant and cherry tomatoes.

Continue to stir over a medium heat, evenly cooking the vegetables and chicken for about 5 minutes. Stir in the Italian seasoning and salt.

As the vegetables continue to cook and more water is released, stir in the tomato paste and red wine vinegar to create a sauce. Once the vegetables are softened and flavorful, about 20 minutes, remove from the heat.

Serve hot with fresh basil and thyme.

APPLE CIDER PORK CHOPS WITH SAGE

Apple and pork are like old friends. This culinary combo is pretty close to perfect, but with the addition of sage and Dijon mustard, it becomes a masterpiece! While this dish may scream fall, it works any time of year. This easy dinner comes together quickly and is one that my family requests often with a side of roasted potatoes.

SERVES 4

4 boneless pork chops, no more than 1 inch (2.5 cm) thick

Kosher salt and ground black pepper

3 tbsp (45 ml) avocado oil or olive oil, divided

½ medium yellow onion, sliced

2 large apples, peeled, cored and cut into ¼-inch (6-mm) slices

3 cloves garlic, minced

¾ cup (180 ml) apple cider

2 tsp (10 ml) Dijon mustard

2 tsp (8 g) arrowroot starch, mixed with 2 tsp (10 ml) water

2 tsp (2 g) chopped fresh sage, for serving

Heat a large skillet to medium-high heat. Season your pork chops on both sides with salt and pepper.

Once the skillet is hot, add 2 tablespoons (30 ml) of oil, then place the pork chops in the skillet. Cook for 4 to 6 minutes per side (4 minutes for ½-inch [1.3-cm] chops and about 6 minutes for 1-inch [2.5-cm] chops), or until browned. The pork chops should be slightly pink on the inside. Remove to a plate and cover with foil.

Now add the remaining tablespoon (15 ml) of oil, and sauté the onion and apples for 3 to 4 minutes. Add the garlic, cook for another minute, then add in the apple cider.

Reduce the heat to medium. Whisk in the mustard, then the arrowroot mixture. Continue to stir, letting the sauce thicken, for about 3 to 4 minutes.

Place the pork chops back into the pan, spooning sauce over the meat. Continue to cook for another few minutes, then remove from the heat.

Serve hot and top with fresh sage.

note: Golden Delicious apples work well in this recipe with their sweet, mellow flavor.

HONEY MUSTARD CHICKEN
AND RAINBOW VEGETABLE STIR-FRY

Let's eat the rainbow, shall we? I'm a girl who loves a good stir-fry; it gives me a good excuse to throw in a variety of vegetables! You can easily substitute your personal favorites, but I've chosen ones that pack in phytonutrients, antioxidants and plenty of crunch. The honey mustard sauce is a fun twist, giving this recipe a salty, sweet and tangy flavor!

SERVES 4

1 cup (240 ml) chicken broth

¼ cup (60 ml) Dijon mustard

2 tbsp (30 ml) gluten-free tamari soy sauce or coconut aminos

2 tbsp (30 ml) honey

2 tbsp (15 g) arrowroot starch

Pinch of crushed red pepper, optional

4 tbsp (60 ml) olive oil or avocado oil, divided

3 cloves garlic, crushed

1 lb (450 g) boneless, skinless chicken breast, cut into 1-inch (2.5-cm) strips

½ cup (75 g) diced white onion

1 cup (150 g) chopped broccolini

1 red bell pepper, sliced

½ cup (75 g) matchstick carrots

½ cup (75 g) diced purple cabbage

1 cup (150 g) chopped Swiss chard

Rice or vegetable noodles, to serve

Kosher salt and ground black pepper, to taste

Fresh basil, to serve, optional

In a small bowl, whisk together the chicken broth, mustard, soy sauce, honey, arrowroot starch and crushed red pepper, if using. Set aside.

Heat a large skillet to medium heat. Once hot, add 2 tablespoons (30 ml) of oil to coat the pan.

Sauté the garlic in oil for 1 minute. Add the chicken and stir-fry until the chicken is no longer pink and is cooked through, about 6 to 8 minutes. Transfer the chicken to a plate.

Add the remaining 2 tablespoons (30 ml) of oil to the hot pan. Slowly add in the vegetables one at a time, about 1 minute apart, and cook for a total of 6 to 8 minutes, or until the veggies are crisp-tender. Add the vegetables in this order: white onion, broccolini, red bell pepper, matchstick carrots, purple cabbage and Swiss chard.

Stir the honey mustard sauce into the vegetables, increase the heat and let thicken for about 1 to 2 minutes. Toss in the chicken and cook until it's heated through, for another 2 to 3 minutes.

Serve over rice or vegetable noodles. Salt and pepper to taste. Garnish with basil, if using.

PERFECT GARLIC BUTTER
FILET MIGNON

My idea of a perfect celebration meal is filet mignon, a glass of red wine and some chocolate. All of it together! This is my "go-to" skillet filet mignon that comes out perfectly every time. It's the one I serve for Christmas dinner (only the best for Jesus), for Valentine's Day and for a birthday celebration. It's a fancy meal that can be made on a busy weeknight but is most special when served for a special occasion. Every kitchen needs a delicious filet mignon method, and this one comes together quickly and pairs well with a vegetable side dish, like my Tangy Skillet Green Beans (page 73). And of course, don't forget the red wine and chocolate!

SERVES 4

4 (6–8-oz [170–227-g]) filet mignon steaks (about 1½–2 inches [3.7–5 cm] thick)

Kosher salt and ground black pepper

2 tbsp (30 g) butter

3 cloves garlic, minced

Bring your filets to room temperature by taking them out of the refrigerator about 45 minutes to an hour before you cook them. Season with a good amount of salt and pepper on each side.

Preheat the oven to 425°F (218°C) and arrange your oven rack in the top third of the oven. On your stovetop, heat a cast iron or ovenproof skillet to high heat.

Add the butter and place the steaks in your pan. Cook for 2 minutes on the first side—do not move them while cooking. Flip to the other side and cook for another 2 minutes. Add the garlic to the pan.

Transfer the skillet to the oven. Let the filets cook for 5 to 6 minutes for medium rare, 6 to 7 minutes for medium, 7 to 8 minutes for medium well and 8 to 9 minutes for well done. These times may vary slightly with different side cuts. If you have a 3-inch (8-cm) filet, add at least a minute to the above times. Do not flip or touch the steaks while they are in the oven!

Remove the steaks from the oven. Transfer to a plate and spoon any additional butter and garlic on top. Season with salt and pepper to taste. Serve hot.

CREAMY MUSTARD TARRAGON CHICKEN WITH MUSHROOMS

When it comes time to serve a nice, elegant dinner that is both simple and delicious, this chicken dish fits the bill! Entertaining should not require hours in the kitchen or an extensive list of ingredients. This has become my "go-to" for dinner parties and is always a crowd pleaser. This classic French dish gets a dairy-free makeover with the addition of coconut milk in place of heavy cream. I love the way the coconut milk complements the Dijon mustard, creating a perfect balance between tangy and slightly sweet.

SERVES 6

3 tbsp (45 ml) avocado oil or olive oil, divided

6 boneless skinless chicken thighs (about 2 lb [907 g]), fat trimmed

Sea salt and ground black pepper

1 shallot, diced

8 oz (227 g) sliced button mushrooms

¾ cup (180 ml) dry white wine

⅓ cup (80 ml) chicken broth

½ cup (120 ml) coconut milk, canned, full-fat

3 tbsp (45 ml) Dijon mustard

3 tbsp (45 ml) fresh chopped tarragon

Vegetables, rice or potatoes, to serve

Heat a large skillet over medium-high heat, and warm 2 tablespoons (30 ml) of oil. Season the chicken thighs with salt and pepper on both sides and add to the skillet. Cook for 5 to 6 minutes per side, or until the chicken is lightly browned and opaque throughout. Transfer the chicken to a plate and cover with foil to keep warm. Do not clean the pan; place it back over the heat.

Heat the remaining tablespoon (15 ml) of oil and add the shallot and mushrooms. Cook until soft, for about 5 minutes. Stir in the wine, scraping any brown bits off the bottom of the pan. Continue to simmer until the liquid begins to reduce, for about 3 minutes. Now add in the broth, coconut milk and Dijon and continue to stir for another 2 minutes. Season with salt and pepper and add in the tarragon.

Return the chicken to the pan, spooning the sauce over the chicken. Let the chicken simmer in the sauce until hot. Transfer to a plate and spoon extra sauce on top. Serve with vegetables, rice or potatoes.

note   This dish does NOT have a coconut taste! In fact, the canned coconut milk is a delicious addition. If you are unsure, you can always omit and use heavy cream in its place.

QUINOA BLACK BEAN
CHEESY ENCHILADA SKILLET

I'd love to welcome the newest member of your Meatless Monday rotation! It's deliciously spiced, packed with protein, filling yet light and bound to become a weeknight staple. Clearly, I have quite a thing for any Mexican-inspired dishes, and this one is my favorite vegetarian dinner! Top with guacamole, salsa, fresh cilantro and everything your heart and belly desires.

SERVES 6

2 tbsp (30 ml) avocado oil or olive oil

½ medium white onion, chopped

2 cloves garlic, minced

1 jalapeño with seeds removed, chopped

2 cups (300 g) frozen corn

2 tsp (5 g) smoked paprika

1 tsp chili powder

1 tsp cumin

½ tsp Kosher salt

2 tbsp (32 g) tomato paste

2 tbsp (30 ml) fresh lime juice

1¾ cups (420 ml) vegetable or chicken broth

1 (14-oz [397-g]) can black beans, drained and rinsed

1 cup (180 g) quinoa, uncooked

1 (14-oz [397-g]) can fire roasted tomatoes

1 cup (120 g) shredded Monterey Jack or pepper jack cheese, optional

1 avocado, sliced for garnish, optional

¼ cup (4 g) chopped fresh cilantro, for garnish, optional

Heat the oven to 425°F (218°C) and arrange the oven rack in the top position.

Heat a large cast iron skillet to medium heat, then coat with oil. Add the onion, garlic, jalapeño and corn. Cook for 5 to 7 minutes, or until fragrant and the onion is translucent.

Meanwhile, in a medium-size bowl, whisk together the paprika, chili powder, cumin, salt, tomato paste, lime juice and broth to form your sauce.

Add the beans, quinoa, canned tomatoes and sauce mixture to your skillet. Mix well and bring to a light boil. Cover with a lid and reduce the heat to a simmer. Keep covered for about 15 to 20 minutes, or until the quinoa has absorbed the liquid and can be fluffed with a fork. If using cheese, cover the quinoa with cheese and place in the oven uncovered for 3 to 5 minutes until bubbly and slightly golden. Serve hot with avocado and cilantro, if desired.

note: This recipe is fantastic heated up and enjoyed throughout the week with a bed of greens.

EASY COQ AU VIN

Let's take a trip to my favorite part of Europe, shall we? The Alsace region is nestled right along the French/German border and is straight out of a scene from *Beauty and the Beast*. Cobblestone streets, French bakeries, French pottery and some of the best wine in the world can all be found in several charming villages. Local cuisine often consists of wine-braised dishes, like a coq au vin. When I am feeling nostalgic for the many memories we made in this charming part of the world or when I want to impress my guests with a fabulous yet simple dinner, coq au vin it is!

SERVES 6

4 thick slices of bacon

3 tbsp (45 ml) olive oil or avocado oil

1 sweet onion, diced

4 cloves garlic, crushed

2 cups (150 g) sliced mushrooms (button, cremini or baby bella)

2 lb (900 g) boneless, skinless chicken breast, diced into 1-inch (2.5-cm) chunks

Kosher salt and ground black pepper

4 medium carrots, cut into ½-inch (1.3-cm) pieces

2 tbsp (32 g) tomato paste

3 cups (720 ml) red wine (Burgundy or zinfandel)

1 cup (240 ml) chicken broth

2 bay leaves

4 sprigs of fresh thyme, for serving

Potatoes or rice, for serving

In a large Dutch oven or deep skillet pan, cook your bacon over medium heat until crispy, about 5 to 7 minutes. Set aside the bacon, remove the bacon grease from the pan and keep the pan hot.

Coat your pan with oil, then toss in the onion. Sauté for 2 to 3 minutes, then add the garlic, mushrooms and chicken. Cook over medium heat, stirring frequently so all sides of the chicken and the mushrooms cook evenly. Cook for about 5 minutes, or until the chicken is almost cooked through. Sprinkle with salt and pepper.

Add the carrots, tomato paste, wine, chicken broth and bay leaves to the pan. Increase the heat to medium-high, and let the mixture bubble for 2 minutes, then reduce the heat to a simmer. Continue to stir occasionally, and cook for another 10 to 12 minutes, or until the sauce thickens.

Remove the bay leaves and add in the fresh thyme. Serve as a stew, or over potatoes or rice. Salt and pepper to taste.

note: You can easily swap out the red wine in favor of a white Riesling during those warmer summer months, or just for a lighter dish.

CAJUN SHRIMP
AND CAULIFLOWER RICE

This lightened-up dish is a twist on the southern classic shrimp and grits! The cauliflower rice makes a great substitute, especially when accompanied with a tangy blend of spices and sautéed vegetables. All you need is twenty minutes of time and a glass of sweetened iced tea to wash it down!

SERVES 4

2 tsp (4 g) smoked paprika

1 tsp Italian seasoning

½ tsp sea salt

½ tsp onion powder

½ tsp garlic powder

¼ tsp cayenne pepper (double for extra heat)

¼ tsp ground black pepper

2 tbsp (30 ml) avocado oil or olive oil, divided

1 tbsp (15 ml) apple cider vinegar

1 lb (450 g) peeled and deveined shrimp

1 large head cauliflower, cored and chopped into florets (about 4 cups [600 g])

½ cup (75 g) diced white onion

1 clove garlic, crushed

1 red bell pepper, diced

2 tbsp (30 ml) water or white wine, optional

2 tbsp (5 g) chopped fresh parsley, for garnish, optional

In a small bowl, mix together the smoked paprika, Italian seasoning, sea salt, onion powder, garlic powder, cayenne pepper and black pepper. Add 1 tablespoon (15 ml) of oil and apple cider vinegar to create a thick sauce. Pour on top of the shrimp and evenly coat. Set aside until ready to use.

Working in batches, place the cauliflower inside a food processor and pulse until it resembles couscous or rice—be careful not to overpulse!

Heat your skillet to medium heat. Coat the pan with the remaining oil, and sauté the onion and garlic for 3 minutes, then add the diced red bell pepper. Continue to cook for another 2 to 3 minutes, then add the cauliflower rice. Sauté the cauliflower rice with veggies for another 5 minutes, or until the rice begins to get lightly toasted.

Add the shrimp with its juices and spices. Continue to stir and mix the veggies, cauliflower rice and shrimp for about 2 minutes. Cover with a lid. If the vegetables seem dry and need more moisture, add water or white wine. Reduce the heat to low, and let the shrimp cook for another 4 to 5 minutes, or until the flesh is slightly opaque and a little white in color.

Garnish with parsley to serve, if using.

TANGY SKILLET GREEN BEANS

Of the many ways to prepare and cook green beans, this cast-iron skillet method takes the cake! The skillet allows the green beans to maintain their crispy texture with a blistering look. The tang of lemon juice and red wine vinegar, paired with browned garlic and crunchy almonds, makes this veggie side dish taste incredible! Since it's made in less than fifteen minutes, this recipe will become a weeknight staple. I can eat this all day during the summer months when green beans are in their peak season. This side also makes a fantastic addition to your holiday spread!

SERVES 4

2 tbsp (30 ml) olive oil or avocado oil

1½ lb (680 g) green beans, washed and trimmed

3 cloves garlic, minced

½ tsp sea salt, plus more to taste

2 tbsp (30 ml) lemon juice

1 tbsp (15 ml) red wine vinegar

⅓ cup (50 g) slivered or chopped almonds

Ground black pepper, to taste

Heat the oil in a large skillet over medium-high heat. Add the green beans and cook, stirring frequently, until the beans begin to blister and brown, about 5 to 7 minutes. Stir in the garlic and salt.

Add in the lemon juice and red wine vinegar, and immediately cover the skillet with a lid. Cook covered for another 2 minutes, or until the green beans are crisp-tender. Remove from the heat.

Top the green beans with the almonds and additional salt and pepper to taste.

PAN-SEARED AHI TUNA WITH PEACH SALSA

Admittedly, I am not a fish person. But tuna filet is a whole different story! I love its meaty texture, and to me, it resembles a filet mignon. This perfectly pan-seared tuna is raw on the inside and tastes so delicious and fresh for a spring or summer meal. The best part? You only need to sear the fish for one to two minutes, making this the ultimate EASY dish!

SERVES 4

1 tsp smoked paprika

½ tsp garlic powder

½ tsp onion powder

½ tsp cayenne pepper

½ tsp oregano

½ tsp sea salt, plus more to taste

¼ tsp ground black pepper

1 lb (450 g) ahi tuna filets, about 1 inch (2.5 cm) thick

2 tbsp (30 ml) olive oil or avocado oil

For the Salsa

1 cup (150 g) diced peaches (about 1–2 peaches)

2 tbsp (20 g) diced red onion

2 tbsp (2 g) chopped fresh cilantro

1 lime, juiced, divided

Heat a skillet to medium-high heat. While the pan is heating, mix together the smoked paprika, garlic powder, onion powder, cayenne pepper, oregano, salt and black pepper in a small bowl.

Rub the seasoning mixture onto both sides of your tuna filets. Once the skillet is very hot, add the oil to coat the pan and then add the filets. Sear for only 1 to 2 minutes per side, so the top is blackened and the middle is still pink and rare.

Next, make your salsa. Stir together the peaches, red onion, cilantro and half of the lime juice.

Slice your tuna and spoon the salsa on top. Squeeze the remaining lime juice over each filet, and season with salt to taste.

CHEESY BRUSCHETTA POLENTA

Polenta is a dish I loved to order out at a restaurant, but never made at home. To my pleasant surprise, it is one of the easiest dishes ever! So now I make it often and love to throw on a ton of veggies for a hearty lunch, side dish or even for a Meatless Monday option. This variation is so simple to throw together, with a deliciously tasty bruschetta topping. It makes a fantastic side dish or dinner!

SERVES 6

1 tbsp (15 ml) olive oil or avocado oil

2 cloves garlic, crushed

4½ cups (1 L) filtered water

1½ cups (240 g) polenta (also labeled as corn meal)

1 tsp sea salt

¾ cup (65 g) Parmesan cheese, divided

For the Bruschetta Topping

1 cup (150 g) diced cherry tomatoes

½ cup (12 g) fresh basil, chopped

2 cloves garlic, crushed

2 tbsp (30 ml) balsamic vinegar or balsamic glaze

Preheat the oven to broil and arrange the oven rack in the top position.

Make the polenta by heating a large skillet to medium heat. Add the oil and garlic, then sauté for 1 to 2 minutes.

Now add the water. Bring to a rolling boil, then slowly pour in the polenta, ½ cup (80 g) at a time. Reduce to a simmer and add the salt. Continue to stir to avoid clumps, and cook for another 3 to 5 minutes, until the water has been absorbed and the polenta is softened. Remove from the heat and stir in ½ cup (45 g) of the Parmesan cheese. Continue to the next step, or as an option, top the polenta with the remaining cheese and let it brown under the broiler for 2 minutes.

Now make your bruschetta topping. In a small bowl, combine the tomatoes, basil and 2 cloves of garlic. Set aside.

Top your polenta with the bruschetta topping, and finally top with balsamic. Spoon into individual bowls and serve hot.

note: Balsamic glaze is a thicker, sweeter and reduced variation of balsamic vinegar. It can be found in most grocery stores.

GROWN-UP GREEN EGGS AND HAM

I've combined three of my top five favorite foods in this dish: eggs, avocado and arugula—foods I eat every day! Scrambled eggs can be kind of tricky and are easily overcooked. The trick is to beat the eggs a ton before adding them to the pan, cook on low heat and remove them from the heat before they are fully cooked. Try my fool-proof method below. I think you'll love the addition of mashed avocado, arugula and prosciutto. The prosciutto is a sophisticated way to enjoy green eggs and ham and happens to pair in the most delicious way with this dish! Feel free to add in some white cheddar cheese or keep it dairy free.

SERVES 2

4 eggs

¼ cup (60 ml) milk (dairy-free is fine)

1 tsp butter or ghee

Kosher salt and ground black pepper, to taste

½ large avocado, mashed

¼ cup (30 g) shredded white cheddar, optional

4 slices prosciutto, cut into small pieces

Handful of fresh arugula

Whisk together the eggs and milk, and continue to beat until the eggs turn one color and are well incorporated. This may take longer than you think, about 2 to 3 minutes!

Heat a large skillet over medium-low heat. Add the butter or ghee, and let it melt. Slowly pour in the egg mixture, letting it set for 30 seconds to 1 minute without letting it brown.

Using a heat-resistant rubber spatula, continue to move the eggs toward the middle, gently tilting the pan and letting the liquid move toward the outside edges of the pan. Add in some salt and pepper. Once the liquid eggs have been cooked through, after about 3 to 4 minutes, turn off the heat. Remove to the side and continue to stir as you add in the mashed avocado so that it's well combined. If using the cheddar, stir it in at this point.

Move to a plate and top with prosciutto and arugula. Serve immediately!

SHAKSHUKA (EGGS IN PURGATORY)

Shakshuka is a traditional Middle Eastern dish with poached eggs in a slightly spicy tomato sauce. I only spent a few days in Israel, and of the many highlights, eating a glorious brunch with Shakshuka for my birthday was certainly unforgettable! So memorable that it has since become one of my favorite dishes for both breakfast and dinner—really because I have a slight obsession with runny eggs. This variation tastes absolutely delicious as is, or you could top it with some feta and serve alongside gluten-free bread.

SERVES 4

2 tbsp (30 ml) avocado oil or olive oil

1 medium sweet onion, diced

1 green pepper, diced

1 clove garlic, minced

2 tsp (5 g) sweet paprika

1 tsp cumin

Pinch of crushed red pepper, optional

½ tsp Kosher salt, plus more to taste

1 (28-oz [790-g]) can whole tomatoes, with liquid

4 large eggs

¼ cup (4 g) chopped parsley or chopped fresh cilantro

Feta cheese or gluten-free bread, for serving, optional

Heat a large ovenproof skillet to medium heat. Coat with oil and toss in the onion. Cook for 3 to 4 minutes until softened, then add the green pepper and garlic. Continue to stir and cook for another 3 minutes.

Sprinkle the paprika, cumin, crushed red pepper (if using) and salt over the vegetable mixture. Then add in the tomatoes with liquid. Continue to cook the mixture for 8 to 10 minutes over medium heat. While the sauce is cooking, set your oven to broil and position your oven rack on the top.

Create 4 wells in the tomato sauce mixture with a wooden spoon. Crack and place an egg in each of the wells. Cover the pan with a lid and reduce the heat to a simmer. Cook for about 5 minutes until the egg whites are almost set.

Remove the lid and place the pan under the broiler for 1 minute, or until the eggs are done to your liking. For a runny, poached egg, remove from broiler after about 1 minute.

Serve hot with the fresh parsley or cilantro along with feta cheese or gluten-free bread, if desired.

MAPLE PECAN BANANA PANCAKES

A healthy stack of pancakes is what Sunday mornings are made for! My daughter is usually in charge of making the family pancakes on the weekends, and this is a recipe we created together. These pancakes are fluffy and lightly sweetened, with all the cozy, comforting flavors we love.

SERVES 4 TO 5

2 large ripe bananas, mashed

3 large eggs

¼ cup (60 ml) milk (dairy-free or your milk of choice)

2 tbsp (30 ml) pure maple syrup

¼ cup (55 g) coconut oil, ghee or butter, plus extra for greasing skillet

1 tsp pure vanilla extract

1½ cups (180 g) blanched almond flour

¼ cup (30 g) arrowroot starch

½ cup (75 g) chopped pecans

½ tsp baking soda

½ tsp baking powder

1 tsp cinnamon

Pinch of sea salt

Butter, to serve

Maple syrup, to serve

Heat a large skillet over medium heat.

In a large bowl, combine the wet ingredients. Beat together the bananas, eggs, milk, maple syrup, coconut oil and vanilla extract.

In a separate bowl, mix together your dry ingredients. Combine the almond flour, arrowroot starch, pecans, baking soda, baking powder, cinnamon and sea salt.

Slowly pour the dry ingredients into the wet ingredients. Whisk well until the batter is smooth and the dry pockets have disappeared. The batter will be pretty thick; you can add water or more milk to thin it out.

Grease your hot skillet with coconut oil, ghee or butter. Slowly pour or spoon the batter into the skillet. Once the edges seem dry and little bubbles begin to form, after about 2 to 3 minutes, flip the pancakes over. You may need to lower the temperature a bit to ensure even cooking without burning. Once the pancakes are firm, after another 2 minutes, remove them from the pan.

Continue until you have used all of the batter. It should make around 8 large pancakes or 1 dozen small to medium-size pancakes. Top with butter and maple syrup to serve!

note: You can also swap in some fresh berries during those warm months. Use just 1 banana and add in ½ cup (74 g) of berries of your choice.

SKILLET CHOCOLATE CHIP COOKIES

A warm and gooey chocolate chip cookie just might be my number one dessert. My mom's chocolate chip cookies were a staple in my household growing up, and she perfected the texture with a gooey middle and slightly golden edge. I've recreated the same texture with my gluten-free and Paleo version using a cast-iron skillet. These are best enjoyed warm right out of the oven with a spoon!

SERVES 4

¼ cup plus 1 tbsp (75 ml) coconut oil, divided

⅓ cup (80 g) smooth almond butter

⅓ cup (48 g) coconut sugar or brown sugar

2 tsp (10 ml) vanilla extract

1 egg

1 cup (120 g) blanched almond flour

¼ cup (30 g) coconut flour

½ tsp sea salt

1 tsp baking soda

½ cup (75 g) chocolate chips or finely chopped chocolate chunks

Preheat the oven to 350°F (177°C) and arrange the oven rack in the center position. Grease an 8-inch (20-cm) cast-iron skillet (or 2 smaller skillets, 3- to 4-inches [8- to 10-cm] each) with 1 tablespoon (15 ml) of coconut oil.

In a medium-size bowl, beat together ¼ cup (60 ml) of coconut oil, almond butter, coconut sugar, vanilla extract and the egg.

In a smaller bowl, whisk together the almond flour, coconut flour, sea salt and baking soda. Pour the dry ingredients into the wet ingredients and continue to fold until well combined. Finally, add in the chocolate chips.

Using a rubber spatula, evenly spread your cookie dough down around the skillet(s). Place the skillet in the oven and bake for 10 to 15 minutes (depending on the oven and size of skillet) until the edges are lightly golden and the middle is just starting to set. Remove the skillet from the oven and let sit for a few minutes.

Spoon directly from the skillet and serve warm!

The INSTANT POT

Have you fallen in love with your Instant Pot yet? It's been all the rage the last few years—for good reason. Sometimes we want a braised meal, hearty soup or stew or saucy ethnic dish that almost always requires several hours, but we want it done fast! The Instant Pot has quickly become my solution for busy weeknights.

Most meals in this chapter would normally take all day but can come together so quickly under "pressure." I stick to only the basic functions of Sauté and Manual, making it even simpler for Instant Pot newbies.

HONEY CHIPOTLE BBQ PULLED CHICKEN WITH APPLE CILANTRO SLAW

What could possibly be more flavorful, easy and versatile than a huge pot of pulled BBQ chicken? Adding chipotle peppers and an apple cilantro slaw to top it off, of course! This is always a huge hit with my kids, and I give plenty of options for serving: a wrap, a bowl, a salad, a pizza, tacos and even as the main feature of "Make Your Own Nachos" night. My favorite way is on top of a bowl of greens or in a lettuce wrap.

SERVES 10

For the Chicken

1 cup (240 ml) chicken broth

1 (6-oz [170-g]) can tomato paste

⅓ cup (80 ml) apple cider vinegar

⅓ cup (80 ml) honey

¼ cup (60 ml) coconut aminos or gluten-free tamari soy sauce

2 chipotles in adobo sauce, chopped

2 tbsp (30 ml) adobo sauce

2 tbsp (30 ml) brown mustard

2 tbsp (30 ml) liquid smoke

2 tsp (10 g) smoked paprika

1 tsp cayenne pepper

½ tsp Kosher salt

3 lb (1.4 kg) boneless, skinless chicken breast

For the Slaw

1 Granny Smith apple, julienned

1 cup (150 g) matchstick carrots

2 cups (680 g) shredded cabbage, red or both red and regular

¼ cup (4 g) chopped fresh cilantro

¼ cup (20 g) chopped green onion

¼ cup (60 ml) avocado oil or olive oil

1 tbsp (15 ml) apple cider vinegar

1 tbsp (15 ml) maple syrup

2 tsp (10 ml) Dijon mustard

1 tbsp (15 ml) sour cream or Greek yogurt, optional

Lettuce wrap, greens or gluten-free tortilla, for serving

Begin by mixing together your sauce in the Instant Pot. Place the broth, tomato paste, apple cider vinegar, honey, coconut aminos, chipotles, adobo sauce, brown mustard, liquid smoke, paprika, cayenne pepper and salt in the Instant Pot and whisk.

Place the chicken on top of the sauce and secure the lid. Select the Manual function, and cook at high pressure for 8 minutes.

While the chicken is cooking, make the slaw. In a medium-size bowl, combine the apple, carrots, cabbage, cilantro and green onion. In a small bowl, whisk together the oil, apple cider vinegar, maple syrup, Dijon mustard and sour cream or Greek yogurt, if using. Pour the dressing over the slaw ingredients and toss to combine.

Once cooking is complete in the Instant Pot, use the Quick Release setting and remove the lid once the steam has been completely released. Shred the chicken with a fork.

Serve in a lettuce wrap with slaw, over a bowl of greens or wrapped in a gluten-free tortilla.

note: With the Instant Pot, this recipe must have a lot of sauce or else it won't come to pressure. My solution to this is using at least 3 pounds (1.4 kg) of chicken. This ensures we have plenty of leftovers for lunches and enough to feed a crowd!

CHILI LIME SALMON
WITH GREEN BEANS

Just four minutes in the Instant Pot for salmon perfection! This might be the easiest dinner in the entire book. This salmon is perfectly tender and flaky, and topped with a delicious honey chili lime sauce! The green beans complete the meal, adding more flavor and nutrient density for a healthy weeknight dinner that can be made in a pinch.

SERVES 3 TO 4

1 cup (240 ml) water

3–4 (4–5-oz [113–142-g]) salmon filets with skin, about 1 inch (2.5 cm) thick

½ tsp seasoned salt or sea salt

Ground black pepper

3 limes, divided

1 tbsp (16 g) tomato paste

2 tsp (10 ml) honey

½ tsp cumin

½ tsp paprika

¼ tsp Kosher salt

Pinch of cayenne pepper, optional

1 tbsp (15 ml) avocado oil or olive oil

8 oz (227 g) green beans, edges trimmed

2 tbsp (2 g) chopped fresh cilantro for garnish, optional

Place the water in the bottom of your Instant Pot. Place the steamer rack on top of the water with the handles extended up.

Season your salmon filets with salt and pepper, and place on top of the steamer rack skin side down.

Cut 1 of the limes into slices, and place the slices on top of the salmon. Secure the lid to your Instant Pot, ensuring the valve is sealed. Select the "Steam" function and adjust the time to 4 minutes. Please note that if the salmon is thicker, you may need to increase the time to 5 or 6 minutes.

While the salmon is cooking, make your chili lime sauce. Juice the remaining 2 limes. Whisk together the lime juice, tomato paste, honey, cumin, paprika, salt and cayenne pepper, if using.

Use Quick Release and once the steam is completely released, remove the lid. Using pot holders, remove the steam rack and salmon from the Instant Pot. Dump the water out and place the pot back inside the Instant Pot.

Select the Sauté function on your Instant Pot. Coat the inside of the pot with oil and place the green beans in the pot. Cook for 3 to 5 minutes or until the green beans are hot, and then press Cancel.

Serve the salmon on top of green beans, spooning the chili lime sauce on top and topped with cilantro, if using.

CHICKEN MARSALA

This dish is everything: succulently creamy, fantastically flavorful and incredibly easy! Although I want to tout its weeknight benefits, it's elegant and sophisticated enough for a Sunday dinner. The Instant Pot creates a fork tender chicken with flavorful mushrooms. Serve alongside a delicious salad and wash it down with a glass of Chardonnay or Pinot Noir!

SERVES 4

2 tbsp (15 g) tapioca starch or arrowroot starch

½ tsp sea salt

Pinch of ground black pepper

½ tsp garlic powder

½ tsp onion powder

4 medium boneless, skinless chicken breast, less than 1 inch (2.5 cm) thick

2 tbsp (30 ml) olive oil or avocado oil

3 tbsp (45 g) butter

½ small sweet onion, diced

3 cloves garlic, minced

8 oz (230 g) sliced baby bella mushrooms

¾ cup (180 ml) high-quality Marsala cooking wine

½ cup (120 ml) chicken broth

⅓ cup (80 ml) heavy cream or coconut cream, optional

Vegetable noodles or rice, for serving

Fresh parsley, for garnish

1 tbsp (3 g) fresh thyme, for garnish

In a small bowl, whisk together the starch, sea salt, black pepper, garlic powder and onion powder. Place the chicken in a sealable bag or container with a lid and add the powdered mix, gently shaking the chicken to evenly coat.

Select the Sauté function on your Instant Pot. Coat the bottom of your pot with oil. Place the chicken inside the pot, and sauté for 1 to 2 minutes per side, or until the chicken has a golden sear. Remove from the pot and set aside.

Now add the butter to the pot and let it melt. Toss in the onion, garlic and mushrooms. Sauté for 3 to 5 minutes, or until the veggies are softened and fragrant. Select Cancel on your Instant Pot, and pour in the wine and chicken broth. Stir the mixture, scraping anything from the bottom of the pot. Place the chicken on top of the wine/mushroom mixture. Secure the lid, ensuring the valve is in the sealed position.

Select Manual on your Instant Pot, and cook on high pressure for 6 minutes. Use the Quick Release; turn the valve to release all the steam before opening the lid.

If using cream, stir it into the mixture. Serve immediately over vegetable noodles or rice. Top with parsley or thyme for garnish.

CREAMY SWEET POTATO, CARROT AND COCONUT SOUP

This soup is a lovely reminder of living in Germany. One of my most treasured memories is homeschooling my daughter and making weekly visits to a small cafe to do homework. During the cold months (generally eight months out of the year!), we loved ordering the creamy carrot soup. It was unbelievably delicious, simple, nourishing and comforting. This variation includes sweet potatoes to create a thicker soup, and the addition of full-fat coconut milk for a dairy-free and creamy taste. This recipe remains one of my daughter's most requested meals!

SERVES 4

2 tbsp (30 g) coconut oil

2 medium yellow onions, diced

4 cloves garlic, minced

2 medium sweet potatoes, peeled and diced into 1-inch (2.5-cm) chunks

12 oz (340 g) carrots, peeled and cut into chunks (about 4 large carrots)

3 cups (720 ml) vegetable broth

1 tsp Kosher salt, plus more to taste

1 (13.5-oz [398-ml]) can full-fat coconut milk

1 tbsp (15 g) fresh thyme, optional

Select the Sauté function on your Instant Pot. Add the oil to the bottom of the pot, and let it heat and melt. Add the onions and garlic. Sauté for 2 to 3 minutes, then select the Cancel function on your Instant Pot.

Place the sweet potatoes, carrots, vegetable broth and salt in the pot. Secure the lid, ensuring the valve is sealed. Select the Manual function and cook on high pressure for 6 minutes.

Once cooking is complete, use the Quick Release. When the steam is completely released, remove the lid.

Now pour in the coconut milk. Blend the soup until completely smooth, using a standard blender or an immersion blender. Add additional salt to taste, and garnish with fresh thyme, if using.

JAMAICAN JERK PULLED PORK

Jamaican Jerk Pulled Pork is incredibly tender, flavorful and company worthy! This twist on pulled pork has a spice combo that is out of this world. I use pork tenderloin because it's leaner, and easier to work with for pulled pork. I love the way it turns out in the Instant Pot, and it's ready in no time!

SERVES 8

2–3 lb (900–1361 g) pork tenderloin (2 individual loins)

2 tsp (5 g) onion powder

2 tsp (5 g) garlic powder

2 tsp (8 g) coconut sugar or brown sugar

1 tsp cinnamon

1 tsp allspice

1 tsp cumin

1 tsp smoked paprika

1 tsp dried thyme

1 tsp dry mustard

½ tsp cayenne pepper

1 tsp Kosher salt

¾ cup (180 ml) pineapple or apple juice

2 tbsp (30 ml) tamari soy sauce

¼ cup (60 ml) apple cider vinegar

¼ cup (60 ml) chicken broth

2 tbsp (30 g) chopped fresh ginger

1 habanero or jalapeño pepper, diced

1 tbsp (8 g) arrowroot starch

1 tbsp (15 ml) water

Rice, gluten-free buns or greens, for serving

Trim off any visible fat from your pork loin and cut each one in half. Pat dry with a paper towel and set aside.

In a small bowl mix together the onion powder, garlic powder, coconut sugar, cinnamon, allspice, cumin, paprika, thyme, dry mustard, cayenne pepper and salt. Generously rub all sides of your pork loin pieces with the spice rub. Reserve any leftover spice for the wet ingredients.

Whisk together the pineapple juice, tamari soy sauce, apple cider vinegar, chicken broth, ginger, habanero or jalapeño pepper and leftover spice rub. You can also blend it together in a food processor or blender.

Place your pork in the bottom of your Instant Pot. Pour the sauce on top of the pork. Secure the lid, ensuring the valve is sealed. Using the Manual function, cook on high pressure for 12 minutes. Use Quick Release when the cook time is over, releasing all the steam before opening the lid.

Remove the pork from the pot and shred with a fork or knife. In a small bowl, whisk together the arrowroot and water. Add the mixture to the Instant Pot to thicken the juices. Place the shredded pork back in the pot. Serve with plenty of sauce over a bed of rice, a gluten-free bun or over a bed of greens.

THAI PUMPKIN CHICKEN CURRY

I cannot pinpoint the very first time I tried chicken curry, but I do know it was love at first bite! Something about a creamy, savory dish packed with veggies and flavor gets me every time. This chicken curry is made in a hurry in the Instant Pot and is sure to become a new weeknight staple. My entire family loves eating this meal, and I enjoy the simplicity and ease of making it! The addition of pumpkin or butternut squash in this dish adds a depth of buttery taste that enhances the flavor. This curry recipe is very mild and not spicy; you can kick it up a few notches with the addition of crushed red pepper!

SERVES 4

2 tbsp (30 ml) avocado oil or olive oil

1 small yellow onion, diced

2 cloves garlic, minced

1 tbsp (10 g) fresh ginger, finely diced

2 cups (300 g) fresh pumpkin or butternut squash, cut into 1-inch (2.5-cm) chunks

1 (14-oz [397-g]) can fire-roasted diced tomatoes, with liquid

3 tbsp (45 ml) red Thai curry paste

¼ cup (60 ml) chicken broth

1 tsp Kosher salt, plus more to taste

2 tsp (10 g) crushed red pepper, optional

1 (14-oz [410-ml]) can full-fat coconut milk, divided

1½ lb (680 g) boneless, skinless chicken breast

2 tbsp (30 ml) lime juice

¼ cup (4 g) chopped fresh cilantro, for garnish

Rice, cauliflower rice or potatoes, for serving

Select the Sauté function on your Instant Pot. Warm up the oil in your pot, then toss in the onion, garlic and ginger. Sauté for just a few minutes, continuing to stir. Select the Cancel button.

Now add in the pumpkin, tomatoes and their liquid, curry paste, chicken broth, salt and crushed red pepper, if using. Poke a hole in the top of the cream portion of your coconut milk and pour only the watery liquid into your pot. Reserve the cream portion of the coconut milk for the end of the recipe. Cut the chicken into bite-sized chunks and add on top of the mixture. Secure the lid, ensuring the valve at the top is sealed. Select the Manual function and cook on high pressure for 8 minutes.

When cooking is complete, use the Quick Release. Once the steam has been completely released, open the lid of your Instant Pot. Stir in the reserved cream portion of your coconut milk and allow it to melt into the mixture. Remove the chicken and cut it into bite-size pieces, or shred with a fork.

Return the chicken to the mixture, add the lime juice and garnish with cilantro, adding salt to taste. Serve over rice, cauliflower rice or potatoes.

note   After cooking and removing the chicken to cut, you can also blend up the sauce with a blender or immersion blender to create a creamy and smooth sauce (great idea for picky eaters!). Then add the chicken back to the sauce prior to serving.

CHEDDAR BROCCOLI POTATO SOUP

This soup will always remind me of the soup that made my little guy a soup fan. For years, I would serve soup at least two nights per week for about eight months out of the year. He would always groan and complain. It wasn't until I loaded up some of his favorite foods—broccoli, cheese and potatoes—that he actually got excited about eating a bowl of soup. He still requests this dinner often, and it has since become a Christmas Eve tradition to eat a bowl of this goodness after church service. It's his favorite night of the year! I love the way the Instant Pot provides a way to make this soup so easily and hands free. Feel free to add some chopped bacon for a loaded variation!

SERVES 4

2 tbsp (30 g) unsalted butter

2 cloves garlic, crushed

4 cups (600 g) broccoli florets

2 lbs (900 g) Yukon Gold potatoes, peeled and cut into small chunks

1 (32-oz [907-ml]) box/can vegetable or chicken broth

1 tsp sea salt

1 tsp ground black pepper

1 cup (240 ml) half-and-half

1 cup (120 g) shredded cheddar cheese

¼ cup (12 g) diced green onion or chives for garnish, optional

Begin by selecting the Sauté button on your Instant Pot. Once the pot is hot, add the butter and garlic. Cook for 1 to 2 minutes until fragrant, then select Cancel.

Add the broccoli, potatoes, broth, salt and pepper to the pot. Secure the lid of your Instant Pot, ensuring the valve is sealed. Now select Manual and cook at high pressure for 5 minutes.

Use the Quick Release, and once the steam is completely released, remove the lid.

Pour the half-and-half into the soup and stir. You can leave the soup chunky or use an immersion blender to puree the broccoli and potatoes.

Serve with cheddar on top, and garnish with green onion or chives, if using.

ORANGE GINGER BEEF AND BROCCOLI

This Asian dish is reminiscent of your favorite take-out dish . . . without the junk ingredients! Orange juice and ginger provide just the right amount of sweetness and heat. I love that you can easily throw together all the ingredients in your Instant Pot for an easy-peasy weeknight dinner. The broccoli is cooked al dente, but if you like your broccoli softer, steam it in the microwave for two minutes before serving.

SERVES 6

½ cup (120 ml) freshly squeezed orange juice

⅓ cup (80 ml) gluten-free tamari soy sauce or coconut aminos

¼ cup (60 ml) rice vinegar

2 tsp (10 ml) sesame oil

2 tsp (10 g) orange zest

3 cloves crushed garlic, divided

3 tsp (15 g) finely chopped fresh ginger, divided

1 tsp crushed red pepper, optional

1 tbsp (15 ml) avocado oil or olive oil

1½ lb (680 g) top sirloin steak, cut into bite-size pieces

3 cups (450 g) chopped broccoli

1 tbsp (8 g) arrowroot starch

1 tbsp (15 ml) water

Rice or cauliflower rice, for serving

2 tsp (10 g) sesame seeds, optional

2 tbsp (12 g) chopped green onion, optional

In a small bowl, whisk together the orange juice, gluten-free tamari soy sauce, rice vinegar, sesame oil, orange zest, 2 cloves of crushed garlic, 2 teaspoons (10 g) of fresh ginger and crushed red pepper, if using. Set the sauce aside.

Select the Sauté function on your Instant Pot. Once hot, add the oil, 1 clove of garlic and 1 teaspoon of chopped ginger. Stir, then add the beef. Cook for 1 to 2 minutes, stirring frequently, until the beef is slightly browned. Select the Cancel function.

Now pour the sauce on top of the beef. Secure the lid, ensuring the valve is in the sealed position. Now select the Manual function and cook on high pressure for 6 minutes.

Once cooking is complete, use the Quick Release. Remove the lid once the steam has been released and toss in the chopped broccoli. Stir, then place the lid back on the Instant Pot to let the broccoli steam and cook for another 3 to 4 minutes.

While the broccoli is steaming, whisk together the arrowroot starch and water in a small bowl. Pour it into the beef and broccoli mixture so the sauce thickens a bit.

Serve over rice or cauliflower rice. Top with sesame seeds and green onion, if using.

SPICY HARISSA CHICKEN AND EGGPLANT

I clearly have an obsession with spicy foods, and harissa is no exception! I had never heard of this famous spice paste until a visit to an African restaurant in my town in Germany. One bite, and I was hooked! It blends a combination of peppers, garlic, oil and vinegar. Harissa sauce is now sold in most grocery stores, making this dish super easy to make. I absolutely love the pairing of harissa with chicken, eggplant and tomatoes served over rice!

SERVINGS 4

¼ cup (60 ml) harissa sauce (see note)

1½ cups (225 g) diced tomatoes

¼ cup (60 ml) fresh lemon juice

1 tsp cumin

1 tsp Kosher salt, plus more to taste

1½ lb (680 g) boneless, skinless chicken, cut into 1-inch (2.5-cm) chunks

1 small eggplant, diced

⅔ cup (160 ml) chicken broth

Rice or cauliflower rice, for serving

3 tbsp (13 g) chopped fresh cilantro for garnish

In your Instant Pot, combine the harissa sauce, tomatoes, lemon juice, cumin and salt. Stir until combined, then add the chicken and eggplant. Pour the chicken broth on top of the mixture.

Secure the lid of your Instant Pot, ensuring the valve is in the sealed position. Select Manual and cook on high pressure for 6 minutes.

Use Quick Release, then remove the lid once all steam has been released. Season with additional salt if needed.

Serve over rice or cauliflower rice with fresh cilantro.

note: You can easily adjust the spice on this recipe by choosing a mild or spicy harissa sauce.

MEXICAN LENTIL SOUP

Of all the different ways to make lentils, this one is my absolute favorite! The Mexican flavors work perfectly with these protein-packed legumes, and this is a recipe that requires very little work! I make this soup often for both a Meatless Monday dinner and for lunches during the week. The salsa verde is an essential ingredient here and can be found in the Mexican aisle of your local grocery store.

SERVES 4

2 tbsp (30 ml) olive oil or avocado oil

1 medium yellow onion, diced

1 jalapeño pepper with seeds removed, diced

1 red bell pepper, diced

2 cloves garlic, minced

1 tbsp (8 g) chili powder

2 tsp (5 g) cumin

½ tsp Kosher salt, plus more to taste

2 cups (360 g) red lentils

1 (14-oz [397-g]) can fire-roasted diced tomatoes

1 cup (240 ml) salsa verde

5 cups (1.2 L) vegetable or chicken broth

Chopped fresh cilantro, optional

Diced avocado, optional

Select the Sauté function on your Instant Pot. Once the pot is hot, coat with the oil and add the onion, jalapeño pepper, red bell pepper and garlic. Sauté for 2 to 3 minutes, until the veggies are softened and fragrant. Select Cancel on the Instant Pot.

Coat the vegetables with the chili powder, cumin and salt. Pour in the lentils, tomatoes, salsa verde and broth. Secure the lid, ensuring the valve is sealed. Select the Manual function and cook on high pressure for 6 minutes. It will take about 10 to 15 minutes for the soup to come to pressure.

Once the cook time is complete, use the Quick Release valve and release all the steam before opening the lid. Serve hot, with optional garnishes.

This soup keeps well in the fridge for up to 1 week or it can be frozen.

INDIAN BUTTER CHICKEN MASALA

It wasn't until I lived in Europe that my love for Indian food developed. I did not grow up eating this fare, although I've always had a love for spicy and very fragrant foods. In Germany, we used to visit a small Indian restaurant in our town where everything was superbly delicious! I have since found a place in my town that is almost as good, and we all love the butter chicken masala. I have tweaked my own recipe several times in my Instant Pot and am very pleased with this dish—I make it all the time! It's very saucy and tastes best the day after it's made. Making it the night before is sometimes easier for me if we have a busy week, but it's not necessary. Bonus: This dinner is always met with enthusiastic smiles!

SERVES 6

2 tbsp (30 ml) coconut oil

4 cloves garlic, minced

1 tbsp (15 g) chopped fresh ginger

1 (14.5-oz [411-g]) can diced tomatoes

2 tsp (5 g) turmeric

2 tsp (5 g) cumin

1 tsp smoked paprika

2 tsp (5 g) garam masala

½ tsp Kosher salt

1 (13.5-oz [399-ml]) can full-fat coconut milk, divided

2 lb (900 g) boneless, skinless chicken breast cut into 1–2-inch (2.5–5-cm) pieces

4 tbsp (60 g) butter, cut into cubes

¼ cup (60 ml) heavy cream, optional

Potatoes, rice or cauliflower rice, for serving

⅔ cup (5 g) chopped fresh cilantro, for garnish

Select the Sauté function on your Instant Pot. Once hot, coat with the oil, then place the garlic and ginger in the pot. Sauté for 1 to 2 minutes until lightly browned, then select Cancel.

Now add the following ingredients into your Instant Pot in this order: the tomatoes, turmeric, cumin, paprika, garam masala, salt and half of the coconut milk. Give the mixture a good stir, then place the chicken on top of the tomato/spice mixture.

Secure the lid on your Instant Pot, ensuring the valve is sealed. Select the Manual function and cook on high pressure for 7 minutes. Use the Quick Release. Once the steam is completely released, remove the lid.

Remove the chicken and set aside. Add the remaining coconut milk, butter and heavy cream (if using) to the pot. Blend the sauce until smooth using an immersion blender or a regular blender. This step is optional, but really enhances the flavors of the sauce! Add the chicken back to the sauce.

Serve over potatoes, rice, cauliflower rice or as is. Garnish with fresh cilantro.

TEXAS THREE MEAT CHILI

My husband, who hates beans, claims that real chili is made with just meat. So, I've been making Texas chili for years, and I'm a convert. The secret to making the best kind of chili is to use different types of meat for texture and flavor, along with a variety of peppers. You would be hard-pressed to find any chili recipe that can be made in thirty minutes, but with the Instant Pot, it's definitely a reality! I still believe that foods like chili taste better the second day, so my favorite way to prepare this recipe is to make it the night before. Or I make it the morning I want to serve it, refrigerate it and then re-heat when ready to eat.

SERVES 8

1 tbsp (15 ml) avocado oil or olive oil

1 medium yellow onion, diced

1 jalapeño pepper with seeds removed, diced

1 poblano pepper, diced

1 red bell pepper, diced

3 cloves garlic, minced

12 oz (340 g) ground beef

12 oz (340 g) top sirloin steak, trimmed of visible fat and diced into chunks

8 oz (227 g) pork sausage

1 (28-oz [794-g]) can whole tomatoes

3 tbsp (24 g) chili powder

1 tbsp (8 g) smoked paprika

1 tbsp (8 g) ground cumin

2 tsp (5 g) chipotle powder, optional

1 tsp Kosher salt, plus more to taste

2 tbsp (32 g) tomato paste

¾ cup (180 ml) gluten-free beer

1 tbsp (15 ml) apple cider vinegar

Toppings

Cilantro

Jalapeños

Cheddar cheese

Onion

Avocado

Select the Sauté function on your Instant Pot. Once hot, coat the bottom of your pot with oil. Cook the onion, jalapeño pepper, poblano pepper and red bell pepper for approximately 3 minutes. Then add in the garlic and cook for another 30 seconds, or until fragrant.

Place the ground beef, steak chunks and sausage into the Instant Pot, and continue to cook for another 5 to 6 minutes. Most of the meat will be browned but doesn't need to be cooked all the way. Select the Cancel function on your Instant Pot.

Add the tomatoes, chili powder, paprika, cumin, chipotle powder (if using), salt and tomato paste. Continue to stir, coating the meat and vegetable mixture with the spices. Pour in the beer and apple cider vinegar. Give it a quick stir and secure the lid. Ensure the valve is sealed on your Instant Pot.

Select the Manual button, and cook on high pressure for 12 minutes.

Use Quick Release, ensuring all steam is released before opening the lid. Give a quick stir and add any additional seasonings and salt. Serve hot with toppings such as cilantro, jalapeños, cheddar, onion or avocado.

The CASSEROLE DISH

The good ol' trusty casserole dish is not just used for Grandma's lasagna. It works wonders even in gluten-free cooking to provide layers of juicy flavors and flavorful sauces!

Any of these recipes can be easily transported to share for a dinner party, potluck or holiday gathering. They will maintain heat best when prepared in a ceramic baking dish.

POMEGRANATE BALSAMIC CHICKEN AND BRUSSELS SPROUTS BAKE

Winner, winner chicken dinner! Let's talk about the flavor combination for this chicken dish: pomegranates, molasses, balsamic vinegar and orange zest all meet for a big high five. Not only is this sauce a perfect companion to chicken, but the sweetness and tang make for the tastiest Brussels sprouts! And with its pretty garnish of pomegranates, oranges and fresh thyme, you can easily see how this dinner is a no-brainer to serve during the holidays.

SERVES 4

⅓ cup (80 ml) pomegranate juice

⅓ cup (80 ml) gluten-free tamari soy sauce

¼ cup (60 ml) balsamic vinegar

2 tbsp (30 ml) blackstrap molasses

3 cloves garlic, minced

2 tsp (10 g) orange zest

Kosher salt and ground black pepper

4 boneless, skinless chicken breasts, pounded to less than 1 inch (2.5 cm) thick

8 oz (227 g) Brussels sprouts, trimmed and sliced in half

Greens, rice or cauliflower rice, for serving

1 tbsp (3 g) fresh thyme, for garnish

⅔ cup (50 g) pomegranate arils, for garnish

Orange wedges, for garnish

Preheat the oven to 375°F (191°C) and arrange the oven rack in the center position.

In a large bowl, whisk together the pomegranate juice, tamari soy sauce, balsamic vinegar, molasses, garlic and orange zest. Salt and pepper your chicken and place inside the bowl to coat (you can also do this step up to 24 hours beforehand and marinate the chicken).

Place the chicken and marinade in a 9 x 13-inch (23 x 33-cm) or 9 x 9-inch (23 x 23-cm) dish. Arrange the Brussels sprouts around the chicken; be sure to brush the marinade over the sprouts.

Bake for 25 to 28 minutes, depending on the thickness of your chicken. Remove from the oven.

Serve hot over a bed of greens, rice or cauliflower rice. Garnish with fresh thyme, pomegranate arils and orange wedges.

MEDITERRANEAN WHITE BEAN–STUFFED ZUCCHINI BOATS WITH GOAT CHEESE

Zucchini boats are everything good in life: healthy, satisfying, affordable and delicious when stuffed with "all the things." While I've made zucchini boats several different ways, I love the way a mashed white bean tastes with fresh herbs, sun-dried tomatoes, olives and topped with goat cheese. A nutritious meal for a Meatless Monday, or even as a healthy lunch!

SERVES 4

3 large zucchini, sliced in half vertically with trimmed edges

1 tbsp (15 ml) olive oil or avocado oil

1 tsp crushed garlic

Kosher salt

1 (15-oz [425-g]) can white beans, drained and rinsed

¼ cup (40 g) diced marinated sun-dried tomatoes, drained

2 tbsp (20 g) chopped red onion

2 tbsp (20 g) chopped Kalamata olives

1 tsp Dijon mustard

1 tsp Italian seasoning

2 oz (57 g) crumbled goat cheese

2 tbsp (5 g) chopped fresh basil, for garnish

2 tbsp (5 g) chopped fresh parsley, for garnish

Preheat the oven to 400°F (204°C) and arrange the oven rack in the center position. Lightly grease a 9 x 13–inch (23 x 33–cm) casserole dish and set aside.

Prepare your zucchini by spooning out the inside. Lightly brush the inside of the zucchini with oil, garlic and a bit of salt.

In a medium-size bowl, mash your white beans. You can also leave some beans whole. Mix in the sun-dried tomatoes, red onion, Kalamata olives, Dijon and Italian seasoning. Spoon the bean mixture evenly into each zucchini boat. Top with the goat cheese, and place foil over the top of your casserole dish.

Bake for 15 minutes, then remove the foil. Cook for another 8 to 10 minutes, or until the goat cheese is bubbly and the zucchini is lightly browned. You can also broil for the final 2 minutes to get everything nice and toasty!

Remove from the oven. Serve and garnish with fresh basil and parsley.

BURRATA AND TOMATO PESTO ZOODLE CASSEROLE

Pasta was once my favorite food to eat. On days that I miss hearty pasta dishes, oodles and oodles of zoodles do the trick! I love the way this all bakes together beautifully with creamy burrata, pesto and fresh garden tomatoes. Take a trip to your local farmers' market and load up on summer's best zucchini and tomatoes. Quality and seasonal vegetables make all the difference in the taste!

SERVES 6

10 medium zucchini, spiralized (about 10–12 cups [1.5–1.8 kg])

1 cup (150 g) cherry tomatoes

2 tsp (8 g) sea salt, plus more to taste

1 cup (240 ml) pesto (see page 166)

½ cup (45 g) freshly grated Parmesan cheese, plus more to taste

8 oz (230 g) burrata cheese

Ground black pepper, to taste

Preheat the oven to 375°F (191°C), and arrange your oven rack in the center position. Grease a 9 x 13–inch (23 x 33–cm) baking dish with cooking spray.

Squeeze any excess moisture out of your zucchini noodles and place them inside your casserole dish. Scatter the cherry tomatoes in with the zoodles. Sprinkle with sea salt, then toss with the pesto to evenly coat the zoodles and tomatoes. Scatter Parmesan cheese across the top.

Transfer to the oven and bake for 20 minutes. Increase the temperature to 400°F (204°C). Remove from the oven and break the burrata over the top of the zoodles, evenly distributing it over the dish. Return to the oven and bake for an additional 8 to 10 minutes, or until the cheese is bubbly.

Serve warm with additional Parmesan if needed, and salt and pepper to taste.

WALNUT-CRUSTED CHICKEN PARMESAN

Chicken Parmesan is one of those meals that never disappoints. My friend Becky introduced me to her "oven-fried" chicken Parmesan over a decade ago, and I loved it. When I made the transition away from gluten, I tested the recipe using pulsed nuts as a bread crumb alternative. It rocked my little dinner world! Nuts provide that perfect crunch, and they mix well with Parmesan cheese and Italian seasoning.

SERVES 4

1 cup (100 g) raw walnuts (or your favorite nut)

¼ cup (22 g) freshly shredded Parmesan cheese, plus more to taste

1 tsp Italian seasoning

½ tsp Kosher salt, plus more to taste

4 cloves garlic, minced

4 tbsp (60 g) unsalted butter or ghee, melted

1 lb (450 g) chicken breast tenders (see note)

2 cups (475 ml) high-quality marinara sauce, such as Rao's

2 tbsp (5 g) fresh basil, for garnish, optional

Preheat the oven to 350°F (177°C) and arrange your oven rack in the center position. Lightly grease a 9 x 13–inch (23 x 33–cm) shallow casserole dish. Set aside.

Using a blender or food processor, pulse together the walnuts, Parmesan cheese, Italian seasoning and salt for about 10 seconds. Do not overpulse. You want the ingredients to be well incorporated, but still have some texture. Place in a shallow bowl.

In a smaller bowl, add the minced garlic to the butter or ghee.

To assemble the dish, dredge each chicken tender in the butter/garlic mixture, then coat with the nut/Parmesan mixture. Place in a single layer in the casserole dish.

Bake for 25 minutes or until the nut coating begins to turn a nice golden brown.

Remove from the oven. Pour the marinara sauce over the chicken. Top with additional Parmesan cheese if desired, and fresh basil to serve, if using.

note: Be sure to use smaller chicken breast tenders as opposed to a large chicken breast, as it makes a difference in the cook time.

GARLIC DILL SALMON

Simple, flavorful, light and deliciously fresh! This salmon is perfectly cooked in a casserole dish, infused with a light white wine and garlic dill flavor. This easy dinner can accompany just about any type of vegetable, salad or even a bed of rice.

SERVES 4

Kosher salt and ground black pepper, to taste

2 lb (900 g) wild-caught salmon filet (about 1 inch [2.5 cm] thick)

2 lemons, divided

4–5 sprigs fresh dill, plus more for garnish

3 cloves garlic, minced

1 tbsp (30 ml) avocado oil or olive oil

¾ cup (180 ml) dry white wine (like a Chardonnay or Sauvignon Blanc)

Preheat the oven to 375°F (190°C) and arrange the oven rack in the center position. Salt and pepper your salmon; set aside.

Cut 1 lemon into slices and arrange them on the bottom of a 9 x 13–inch (23 x 33–cm) casserole dish. Place the dill sprigs on top of the lemon. Now place the salmon (skin side down) on top of the lemon and dill.

In a small bowl, whisk together the juice of half the other lemon, garlic and oil. Brush the mixture over the salmon. Pour the white wine over the salmon. Place a piece of foil on top of the casserole dish.

Bake for 18 to 25 minutes, depending on the thickness of your salmon. Check after 18 minutes to see if the top is firm and the salmon can be easily flaked with a fork. Alternatively, use a thermometer and ensure the internal temperature at the thickest part of your salmon is 145°F (63°C).

PROSCIUTTO-WRAPPED MAPLE MUSTARD CHICKEN

Maple mustard sauce is always a great idea for chicken, but pair it with salty prosciutto and fresh basil, and it's a winner every time! This is a meal that is on a permanent weeknight rotation in my kitchen, and one that is an absolute breeze to make.

SERVES 4 TO 6

2 tbsp (30 ml) whole grain Dijon mustard

2 tbsp (30 ml) white wine vinegar

2 tbsp (30 ml) real maple syrup

Kosher salt and ground black pepper

4–6 chicken cutlets, less than 1 inch (2.5 cm) thick (see note)

Handful of basil leaves

4–6 slices prosciutto

1 tbsp (8 g) arrowroot starch, optional

1 tbsp (15 ml) cold water, optional

Rice, greens or potatoes, for serving

Preheat the oven to 375°F (191°C) and arrange the oven rack in the center position.

In a small bowl, whisk together the whole grain Dijon mustard, white wine vinegar and maple syrup.

Salt and pepper each chicken cutlet. Brush each cutlet with the mustard, vinegar and maple sauce, top with 1 or 2 fresh basil leaves, then wrap each cutlet with a slice of prosciutto. Arrange each piece of chicken in your pan and pour the remaining sauce over the chicken.

Bake for 22 to 24 minutes, or until the chicken is completely cooked. Remove from the oven.

Whisk together the arrowroot starch and water and add it if you would like to thicken the sauce. Serve each piece of chicken by spooning extra sauce on top over a bed of rice, greens or potatoes.

note: This recipe requires cutlets less than 1 inch (2.5 cm) thick for a faster cook time!

PEAR AND APPLE CRISP

When I first met my husband, he told me his favorite dessert was an apple crisp. Huh? I was born and raised a chocoholic and never understood fruit for dessert. But in an effort to impress him in those early dating days, I did the unthinkable: I made my first dessert without chocolate. Although this gluten-free version is much different than the original one, I think it's much tastier, healthier and—dare I say—just as good as a chocolate dessert! My husband and daughter both love the pear combo for a fall treat. It's also a cinch to make!

SERVES 8

For the Filling

2 cups (300 g) diced, peeled and cored apples

2 cups (300 g) diced, peeled and cored pears

1 tbsp (15 ml) lemon juice

1 tsp cinnamon

1 tbsp (13 g) coconut sugar

¼ cup (60 ml) canned coconut milk

2 tbsp (30 ml) real maple syrup

For the Topping

¾ cup (55 g) chopped pecans or walnuts

¼ cup (30 g) almond flour

1 tbsp (13 g) coconut sugar

1 tsp cinnamon

Pinch of Kosher salt

2 tbsp (30 ml) coconut oil

Preheat the oven to 375°F (191°C) and arrange the oven rack in the center position. Lightly grease an 8 x 8-inch (20 x 20-cm) casserole dish.

For the filling, place the apples and pears inside your casserole dish and toss with lemon juice.

In a smaller bowl, mix together the cinnamon, coconut sugar, canned coconut milk and maple syrup. Pour over the apples and pears, evenly coating the fruit.

In another small bowl, mix together your crumb topping. Combine the chopped pecans, almond flour, coconut sugar, cinnamon and salt. Then fold in the coconut oil and spoon the topping over the apples and pears.

Place the dish in the oven and bake for 20 to 25 minutes, or until the fruit is bubbling and the crisp topping is golden. Serve hot.

This dish can also be refrigerated for up to a week and reheated.

note: Gala, Braeburn or Honeycrisp apples work well as baking apples. Bosc or Anjou pears work best and will hold their shape in this crisp.

TRIPLE BERRY AND LEMON COBBLER

For those spring and summer days when berries are at their peak, what better use for them than a sweet cobbler? Topped with buttery and nutty flavored biscuits and lemon-infused flavors, this cobbler is definitely a dessert I will happily, and without guilt, cheat on chocolate for! A whipped topping or ice cream is optional, but kind of necessary.

SERVES 8

3 cups (450 g) halved strawberries

2 cups (250 g) raspberries

1 cup (150 g) blueberries

⅓ cup (65 g) coconut sugar, divided

2 tbsp (30 ml) lemon juice

¼ cup (30 g) arrowroot starch, divided

¾ cup (30 g) blanched almond flour

2 tsp (10 g) lemon zest

¼ tsp sea salt

½ tsp baking soda

½ cup (120 ml) coconut oil, melted

1 tsp lemon extract

2 tbsp (30 ml) milk or dairy-free milk

Ice cream or whipped cream, for topping, optional

Preheat the oven to 375°F (191°C) and arrange your oven rack in the center position. Lightly grease a 9 x 13–inch (23 x 33–cm) casserole dish.

In a large bowl, combine the strawberries, raspberries, blueberries, 1 tablespoon (13 g) of coconut sugar, lemon juice and 1 tablespoon (8 g) of arrowroot starch. Toss gently, then pour into the prepared dish.

In a separate bowl, combine the remaining arrowroot starch, almond flour, lemon zest, remaining coconut sugar, sea salt and baking soda. Add in the coconut oil, lemon extract and milk and mix with a wooden spoon to form a thick dough.

Divide the dough into 4 to 6 equal parts and flatten. Place on top of the berry cobbler. Transfer your dish to the oven. Bake for 28 to 30 minutes, or until bubbly and the biscuit mixture is lightly browned.

Serve warm. Top with optional ice cream or whipped cream.

The SOUP POT

If there was ever a dish I could eat for every meal, it would most definitely be soup. I love a hearty, warm bowl of veggies and protein to fill me up without being too heavy. It's also the food I love to serve when entertaining! It's easy to control the temperature and requires little work once guests arrive. My stockpot is one of the dishes used most in my kitchen.

SPICY CHICKEN ZOODLE SOUP

Zippy—that's how I describe this yummy soup. Chicken noodle soup has always been a favorite, and with the addition of zucchini noodles and buffalo hot sauce, I elevated this soup to a whole new level! It's low carb and just downright delicious. I love this hot soup as an easy lunch to enjoy throughout the week, or as dinner on a cold winter night.

SERVES 6

2 tbsp (30 ml) avocado oil or olive oil

1 medium yellow onion, diced

1 lb (450 g) boneless, skinless chicken breast, cut into bite-size pieces

1 tsp Kosher salt

½ tsp ground black pepper

3 stalks celery, diced (about 1 cup [128 g])

4 large carrots, peeled and diced (about 1 cup [128 g])

40 oz (1.2 L) chicken broth

¼–½ cup (60–120 ml) buffalo hot sauce (see note)

3 cups (420 g) zucchini noodles

¼ cup (4 g) fresh cilantro, chopped, optional

Heat a large stock pot to medium heat. Once hot, add the oil and sauté the onion for 3 minutes.

Place the chicken, salt and pepper into the pot. Sauté with the onion for another 3 to 4 minutes. Add the celery, carrots, chicken broth and hot sauce. Bring to a boil, reduce the heat to a simmer and add the zucchini noodles.

Let simmer for another 5 to 7 minutes before serving. Garnish with fresh cilantro, if using.

note This recipe is pretty spicy with ½ cup (120 ml) of hot sauce. Start with ¼ cup (60 ml) and adjust to taste.

TURMERIC BLACK BEAN
AND SWEET POTATO SOUP

I call this the anti-inflammatory soup. It's basically a bowl full of functional foods and nutrients, and although the pairings of these foods may not seem to make sense at first, they work deliciously well! An infusion of Asian and Mexican flavors, this soup is sure to delight your taste buds!

SERVES 6

2 tbsp (30 ml) avocado oil or olive oil

1 small sweet onion, diced

1 tbsp (10 g) finely chopped fresh ginger

2 cups (270 g) diced sweet potatoes

2 (14-oz [399-g]) cans black beans, drained and rinsed

1 (14-oz [399-g]) can diced tomatoes, with liquid

2 tsp (4 g) ground turmeric

1 tsp ground cumin

1 tsp sea salt, plus more to taste

3 cups (700 ml) vegetable broth

1 cup (240 ml) full-fat coconut milk

Juice of 2 limes

¼ cup (4 g) chopped fresh cilantro

Heat a large stockpot to medium heat. Coat the bottom with oil, then toss in the onion, ginger and sweet potatoes. Cook for 4 to 5 minutes, or until fragrant.

Add the black beans, tomatoes with liquid, turmeric, cumin and salt. Stir until the ingredients are combined, then add your vegetable broth.

Bring the soup to a slight boil, then reduce the heat to a simmer. Let simmer for 10 to 12 minutes, letting the flavors develop. Pour in the coconut milk and stir so that it melts in the soup. Add the juice of the limes to the pot.

Serve hot, and top with fresh cilantro and more salt to taste.

GROUND TURKEY TACO SOUP

I remember my mom making only a few dishes growing up—she'll be the first to admit she was not much of a cook. Taco soup was her forté, and being the taco connoisseur that I am, it was my favorite dinner! I have changed her version over the years and substitute ground turkey in this flavorful dish. This is a lightning fast version that really can be done in twenty minutes. My husband is the biggest taco soup fan you will ever meet, and since he has an aversion to beans, they are omitted in this soup. Feel free to add in some black beans for some additional protein. The avocado and chopped fresh cilantro are optional, but definitely worth it!

SERVES 4

1 tbsp (15 ml) olive oil or avocado oil

1 medium sweet onion, diced

1 jalapeño pepper with seeds removed, diced

1 orange bell pepper, diced

1 lb (450 g) ground turkey

2 tsp (4 g) ground cumin

2 tsp (4 g) smoked paprika

1 tsp chipotle chili powder

1 tsp chili powder

½ tsp Kosher salt, plus more to taste

1 (14-oz [397-g]) can fire-roasted diced tomatoes, with liquid

1 (14-oz [410-ml]) can diced green chilis, with liquid

5 cups (1.2 L) chicken broth

Juice of 1 lime

1 avocado, diced, for garnish, optional

¼ cup (4 g) chopped fresh cilantro, for garnish, optional

Heat a large stockpot or Dutch oven to medium heat. Once hot, coat the bottom with oil. Add the onion and cook for 3 minutes until fragrant.

Toss in the jalapeño, orange bell pepper and ground turkey. Cook until the turkey is no longer pink, continuing to stir the veggies and turkey in the pan, about 5 to 6 minutes.

Add the cumin, paprika, chipotle powder, chili powder and salt to the veggie/turkey mixture and mix until the spices are well combined. Then add the tomatoes, chilis and chicken broth.

Adjust the heat to medium-high for 3 minutes, then reduce the heat to a simmer. Simmer for 5 to 10 minutes until ready to serve. Salt to taste and add the lime juice before ladling the soup into individual bowls.

Top with avocado and fresh cilantro, if using.

JALAPEÑO POPPER WHITE CHICKEN CHILI

White chicken chili is one of my favorite meals in the colder months. This jalapeño popper version is a fun twist on the classic dish with chopped bacon and diced jalapeño that is sure to please a crowd. It makes a great dish for a snow day, football season or even a chili cook-off! Don't forget to slather on the toppings: cilantro, chopped tomatoes, cheddar cheese and even pickled jalapeños are all delicious companions.

SERVES 8

6 slices of bacon

1 white onion, diced

2 jalapeño peppers with seeds removed, diced

2 tsp (5 g) chili powder

1 tsp ground cumin

½ tsp cayenne pepper

½ tsp Kosher salt, plus more to taste

2 tbsp (15 g) arrowroot starch

2 cups (475 ml) chicken broth

2 (14-oz [397-g)] cans navy beans or great northern beans, drained and rinsed

3 cups (375 g) shredded rotisserie chicken (see note)

2 (4-oz [113-g]) cans diced green chilis

8 oz (227 g) cream cheese, softened

Optional Toppings

Chopped fresh cilantro

Shredded cheddar cheese

Chopped tomatoes

Pickled jalapeños

Heat a large stockpot to medium-high heat. Add the bacon to the hot pan, and cook for 2 to 3 minutes per side, or until desired crispiness. Remove the bacon and set aside to cool, then crumble. Keep 2 tablespoons (30 ml) of bacon fat in the pot; do not turn off the heat on the stove.

Add the onion and jalapeños to the stockpot. Cook for 4 to 5 minutes, or until softened and fragrant. Add the chili powder, cumin, cayenne pepper and salt to the vegetable mix.

Mix the arrowroot starch into the chicken broth and add to the vegetable mix. Mix in the beans, chicken, chilis and cream cheese. Bring the mixture to a boil, then reduce the heat to a simmer so it begins to thicken. Continue to simmer for 10 to 15 minutes, stirring occasionally, letting the cream cheese melt and chili flavor develop.

Spoon into individual bowls while hot, and top with crumbled bacon. Add any desired additional toppings.

note Rotisserie chicken is used in this recipe for convenience and to keep the cook time under 30 minutes, but any shredded chicken will work. You can cook 1 pound (450 g) of chicken breast or thighs to get approximately 3 cups (660 g) of shredded chicken.

LASAGNA SOUP
WITH ZUCCHINI NOODLES

Lasagna is one of those time-consuming dishes that I've never been too crazy about eating or preparing. Throwing the same ingredients into a big pot to create a soup, however, is totally up my alley! I love that you still get that same taste, without the additional work. Plus, this soup variation is much lighter than its casserole form. It's easily one of my entire family's favorites in the colder months!

SERVES 8

2 tbsp (30 ml) avocado oil or olive oil

1 medium yellow onion, diced

2 large cloves garlic, minced

8 oz (227 g) ground beef

8 oz (227 g) Italian sausage

1 (28-oz [794-g]) can of diced tomatoes, with liquid

1 tsp dried oregano

1 tsp dried basil

1 tsp Kosher salt, plus more to taste

½ tsp crushed red pepper, optional

3 tbsp (49 g) tomato paste

32 oz (950 ml) chicken broth

2 medium zucchini, spiraled

½ cup (60 g) ricotta cheese

½ cup (45 g) Parmesan cheese, for serving, optional

¼ cup (6 g) fresh basil, chopped

Begin by heating a large stockpot to medium-high heat. Once hot, add the oil, onion and garlic. Cook for approximately 2 to 3 minutes until fragrant, then reduce the heat to medium.

Now add in the beef and sausage, cooking until no longer pink, for about 5 to 6 minutes.

Add in the tomatoes with liquid, oregano, basil, salt, crushed red pepper (if using), tomato paste and broth and bring to a boil. Once boiling, add in the zucchini noodles. Reduce the heat to a simmer, and cook until the noodles are softened, about 3 to 4 minutes.

Stir in the ricotta cheese, and salt to taste. Pour the soup into individual bowls while hot. Garnish with Parmesan, if using, and a sprinkle of basil to each bowl.

CURRY LIME CHICKPEA STEW

Unconditional love and a giant comfort hug in one bowl. Whatever life may be throwing at you, this soup is sure to nourish the body and the soul! I first developed this soup several years ago for a friend who was visiting and going through a tough time. It still remains a favorite of hers and mine! It has a healthy amount of spices without being too spicy, and it's finished off with some lime for a great tangy punch! And let's not forget about the veggies. Packed with a variety of textures and tastes, I am confident this will become a new staple during soup season.

SERVES 3 TO 4

1 tbsp (15 g) coconut oil

1 small yellow or white onion, diced

2 tbsp (30 g) fresh ginger, chopped

1 large clove garlic, minced

1 red bell pepper, chopped

1 large sweet potato, skinned and chopped into small ½-inch (1.3-cm) pieces

1 cup (150 g) cherry tomatoes, chopped

3 tbsp (45 g) red Thai curry paste

24 oz (700 ml) vegetable broth

1 (14-oz [410-ml]) can full-fat coconut milk

1 (14-oz [397-g]) can chickpeas, drained and rinsed

Juice of 3 limes

Fresh cilantro, for garnish, optional

Begin by heating a large pot to medium-high heat on your stovetop. Add the coconut oil and let it melt.

Add in the onion, ginger, garlic, red bell pepper and sweet potato. Cook the vegetables for 6 to 8 minutes, until the sweet potato is soft and the onion is clear. Then add the tomatoes.

Coat the vegetables with curry paste, and then pour in the vegetable broth. Reduce the heat to medium, then add in the coconut milk and chickpeas. Let the coconut milk melt and blend in with the soup. Simmer for 10 to 15 minutes so the flavors can meld.

Before serving, add the lime juice to your soup. Garnish with fresh cilantro, if using.

CAULIFLOWER AND CHORIZO CORN CHOWDER

I call this dish, "my favorite mistake." This was developed during a snowstorm when I couldn't get to the store and had to use whatever was in my fridge. Oh yeah, and I was determined to make it a soup. This chowder is veggie-packed and has a slightly spicy and tangy taste. Veggies can be swapped out; I've made this chowder many times with diced potatoes instead of cauliflower.

SERVES 4

2 tbsp (30 ml) avocado oil or olive oil

1 medium sweet onion, diced

2 cups (200 g) cauliflower, chopped

1 cup (150 g) frozen corn

1 red bell pepper, diced

3 cloves garlic, minced

1 lb (450 g) chorizo sausage or spicy Italian sausage (see note)

32 oz (950 ml) chicken broth

¼ cup (60 ml) pepperoncini juice

1 tbsp (15 ml) hot sauce

½ cup (120 ml) half-and-half

1 tbsp (15 ml) fresh lime juice

¼ cup (4 g) fresh cilantro, chopped

Heat a large stockpot to medium heat and add the oil to coat the pot. Toss in the onion, cauliflower and frozen corn and cook for 3 to 4 minutes, until the veggies begin to soften.

Next, add the red bell pepper, garlic and sausage to the pot. Cook for another 5 to 6 minutes, or until the sausage is almost cooked through.

Pour the chicken broth, pepperoncini juice and hot sauce into the pot. Increase the heat to medium-high for 5 minutes, then reduce to a simmer. Let simmer for 8 to 10 minutes. Add in the half-and-half and lime juice, then remove from the heat.

Serve hot with fresh cilantro on top.

note: Not all sausage is gluten-free, so be sure to check the labels!

The
MUFFIN PAN

Breakfast, lunch, dessert and even dinner—the muffin pan does it all! These perfectly portioned recipes are all perfect for meal prep on the weekends and make great freezable meals to enjoy throughout the week. I use most of these recipes as lunchbox main courses for school lunches and as meal solutions for busy weekdays.

PEANUT BUTTER AND JELLY BANANA MUFFINS

Pure breakfast brilliance. This good ole classic combo makes the most scrumptious, fluffy and tasty muffin ever! At any given time, you can usually find a stash of these muffins in my freezer. I love to bake them ahead on weekends and defrost them to use in my kids' lunch boxes or for breakfast.

SERVES 12

2 cups (240 g) blanched almond flour

1 tsp cinnamon

1 tsp baking soda

½ cup (129 g) smooth peanut butter

¼ cup (60 ml) raw honey

3 large eggs

2 ripe bananas, mashed

⅔ cup (80 ml) jam

1 banana, sliced into 12 slices

Preheat the oven to 350ºF (177ºC) and arrange the oven rack in the center position. Grease a 12-cup muffin pan or line with cupcake liners. Set aside.

In a medium-size bowl, mix together the almond flour, cinnamon and baking soda.

In a large bowl, mix together the peanut butter, honey and eggs. Beat until smooth, then fold in the mashed bananas.

Slowly add the dry ingredients to the wet ingredients, continuing to mix until the dry flour pockets disappear.

Fill your muffin cups to ½ full. Spoon a teaspoon of jam into each cup, then top with another scoop of muffin batter (so the muffin cups are about ¾ full). Add a banana slice to the top of each muffin.

Bake for 16 to 18 minutes or until the top is spongy and lightly browned. Remove the muffins from the oven and let cool for 7 to 10 minutes.

STRAWBERRY BANANA N'OATMEAL CUPS WITH CHOCOLATE CHIPS

Portable, easy, nutritious and delicious. A winning breakfast combo! These cups are reminiscent of baked oatmeal cups, but without any grains. Packed with healthy fats and protein, these are sure to nourish your belly to start the morning. The oatmeal-like texture of these grain-free N'Oatmeal Cups is a favorite to give to my kids for an on-the-go breakfast on a busy weekday, or as a lunchbox treat.

SERVES 12

2 cups (240 g) shredded coconut

1 cup (150 g) chopped pecans

2 tbsp (15 g) coconut flour

1 tsp baking soda

1 tsp cinnamon

½ tsp Kosher salt

½ cup (75 g) chocolate chips

4 eggs, whisked

¾ cup (180 ml) dairy-free milk (such as almond or flax)

2 ripe bananas, mashed

1 tbsp (15 ml) vanilla extract

2 tbsp (30 ml) real maple syrup

¾ cup (110 g) diced strawberries

Preheat the oven to 350°F (177°C) and arrange the rack in the center position. Lightly grease a 12-cup muffin tin, or line with cupcake liners. Set aside.

In a medium-size bowl, mix together the shredded coconut, pecans, coconut flour, baking soda, cinnamon, salt and chocolate chips.

In a larger bowl, whisk together the eggs, milk, bananas, vanilla and maple syrup.

Fold the dry ingredients into the wet ingredients, then gently add the strawberries. Scoop the mixture into the muffin cups, filling to the top.

Place the N'oatmeal cups in the oven and bake for 22 to 24 minutes, depending on the oven. Let cool for a few minutes in the pan before removing.

SOUTHWEST EGG MUFFINS

Breakfast, lunch or dinner? I just love a dish that can be enjoyed for any meal! These hearty muffins pack a protein punch and make a great on-the-go breakfast or snack. I love to prep these on the weekend and keep them on hand to enjoy throughout the week! You can easily make this dairy-free by omitting the cheese and using a dairy-free milk.

SERVES 12

10 large eggs

½ cup (120 ml) milk (or dairy-free milk)

1 tsp sea salt

1 tsp smoked paprika

½ tsp ground cumin

½ cup (90 g) canned black beans, drained and rinsed

⅔ cup (50 g) diced tomatoes

3 tbsp (3 g) chopped fresh cilantro

2 tbsp (20 g) chopped green onion

1 small jalapeño pepper with seeds removed, diced

½ cup (60 g) shredded cheddar cheese, optional

Preheat the oven to 375°F (191°C) and arrange your oven rack in the center position. Lightly grease a 12-cup muffin pan and set aside.

In a large bowl, whisk together the eggs, milk, salt, paprika and cumin.

In a smaller bowl, stir together the black beans, tomatoes, cilantro, onion and jalapeño.

Pour the egg mixture evenly into the muffin cups, filling almost to the top. Then spoon about 1 tablespoon (11 g) of the black bean mixture into each muffin cup. Top each muffin with cheese, if using.

Place in the oven and bake for approximately 22 minutes, or until the top is lightly browned and the egg is firm. Remove the muffins from the oven and let cool for a few minutes before removing from the pan.

The muffins can be stored in the refrigerator for up to 1 week, or frozen for up to 3 months.

MEATLOAF MUFFINS

Not your old-fashioned meatloaf! These mini versions are packed with flavor and veggies, cook faster and are so much easier to serve! These gems always get my kids running to the dinner table and ready to devour. Serve with a side of potatoes, vegetables or even my Skillet Cheesy Bruschetta Polenta (page 77) for a comforting Sunday evening dinner.

SERVES 6

For the Meatloaf

1 lb (450 g) grass-fed ground beef or turkey

1 lb (450 g) Italian sausage

⅔ cup (100 g) diced white onion

2 cloves garlic, minced

2 tsp (5 g) Italian seasoning

½ tsp Kosher salt

2 eggs

¼ cup (60 ml) coconut aminos or gluten-free tamari soy sauce

1 tsp Dijon mustard

¼ cup (30 g) coconut flour

For the Tomato Topping (see note)

4 tbsp (65 g) tomato paste

2 tbsp (30 ml) apple cider vinegar

1 tsp ground mustard

1 tsp smoked paprika

1 tsp raw honey

½ tsp garlic powder

½ tsp onion powder

Preheat the oven to 350°F (177°C) and arrange the oven rack to the center. Lightly grease a 12-cup muffin pan and set aside.

In a large bowl, mix together the beef, sausage, onion, garlic, Italian seasoning and salt.

In a smaller bowl, whisk the eggs with the coconut aminos and mustard. Pour into the beef mixture and continue to mix until well combined. Then fold in the coconut flour to absorb some of the moisture.

For the tomato topping, in another bowl, whisk together the tomato paste, apple cider vinegar, mustard, paprika, honey, garlic powder and onion powder.

Scoop the meat mixture into each muffin cup, filling to the top. Spoon the tomato topping over each muffin, smoothing out to cover.

Bake for 22 to 24 minutes, or until the muffins are cooked through. Remove from the oven and puncture each muffin with a fork.

note: You can omit the tomato topping and replace it with your personal preference for gluten-free ketchup.

CHAI-SPICED APPLE DONUT HOLES

I am constantly creating new and fun baked breakfast treats for my kids that are also dense in nutrients. These donut holes are one of their favorites. I love them because they are packed with healthy fats and protein and can be made ahead on the weekends to be enjoyed throughout the week. I love portable food for those busy school mornings! Bonus: They also make a delicious afternoon snack with a cup of coffee or tea for us adults. The coconut sugar makes these bites refined-sugar-free and Paleo, but can easily be swapped out with granulated sugar.

SERVES 12

For the Donut Holes

¾ cup (90 g) blanched almond flour

¼ cup (30 g) coconut flour

1 tsp cinnamon

½ tsp ground ginger

¼ tsp cardamom

¼ tsp cloves

½ tsp baking soda

¼ tsp Kosher salt

2 eggs

⅓ cup (80 ml) apple sauce

1 tsp vanilla extract

2 tbsp (30 ml) maple syrup

For the Topping (optional)

⅓ cup (65 g) coconut sugar or granulated sugar

1 tsp cinnamon

½ tsp ground ginger

¼ tsp cardamom

¼ tsp cloves

¼ cup (60 ml) coconut oil, melted

Preheat the oven to 350ºF (177ºC) and arrange the oven rack in the center position. Lightly grease a 24-mini-muffin tin with a nonstick spray. Set aside.

In a large bowl, combine the flours, cinnamon, ginger, cardamom, cloves, baking soda and salt. Mix well.

In a smaller bowl, whisk together the eggs. Then add the apple sauce, vanilla and maple syrup. Add the wet ingredients to the dry ingredients and continue to mix with a wooden spoon until the batter is well combined.

Scoop the batter into the muffin tin, filling each cup almost to the top. Smooth the top of each muffin cup. Transfer to the oven and bake for 12 to 14 minutes (depending on the oven). Remove and set aside to cool for a few minutes.

While cooling, for the topping, mix together the sugar, cinnamon, ginger, cardamom and cloves. Dip each donut hole in coconut oil, then into the sugar mixture. Set aside on parchment paper.

note: Enjoy warm, or store in an airtight container for up to 3 days. These can also be frozen for up to 1 month and defrosted to eat.

BROWNIE BITES

I'm a chocoholic. Brownies and chocolate cake are my two favorite desserts, and these little bites are something I always keep on hand for those chocolate cravings! I love their little size, perfect so that I don't accidentally overindulge. They also are great nibbles for little bellies and an easy recipe for kids to practice their baking skills!

SERVES 12

1 cup (120 g) almond flour

½ cup (50 g) cocoa powder

½ tsp baking soda

¼ tsp sea salt

3 eggs

½ cup (120 ml) coconut oil, melted

⅓ cup (80 ml) raw honey

1 tsp vanilla extract

½ cup (75 g) chocolate chips

Preheat the oven to 350°F (177°C) and arrange the oven rack in the center position. Lightly grease a 24-mini-muffin tin with a nonstick spray and set aside.

In a large bowl, mix together the almond flour, cocoa powder, baking soda and salt.

In a smaller bowl, whisk together the eggs, coconut oil, honey and vanilla. Dump the wet ingredients into the dry ingredient bowl and mix well with a wooden spoon until no dry pockets remain. Fold in the chocolate chips.

Spoon the brownie mixture into the muffin cups, filling each cup to the top. Transfer to the oven and bake for 13 to 15 minutes, or until the tops have risen and the brownies feel firm to the touch.

Remove from the oven and let sit for 5 minutes before removing from the pan.

This can be stored in an airtight container for up to 1 week, or frozen for up to 1 month.

The BLENDER

Smoothies, salads, soup, sauces and dessert. So many options with my favorite kitchen gadget! This is the chapter that requires no cooking, but is still full of tasty recipes. It's also the home to my most frequently made recipes and ones that I make each and every week.

THE FOUR SEASONS SALAD

This recipe is for my super chic, classy, champagne-loving, and hostess-with-the-mostest friend, Janae. She asked me for a "go-to" salad that she can serve for any occasion or holiday when entertaining. I came up with the idea to customize a salad with the same base dressing, adapted with tasty seasonal specialties to suit every occasion, any time of the year. Be the friend who always serves the best salads!

SERVES 4

For the Dressing

Zest of 1 lemon (see note)

¼ cup (60 ml) fresh lemon juice (see note)

2 tbsp (30 ml) honey

1 tbsp (15 ml) Dijon mustard

1 tbsp (15 ml) red wine vinegar

1 clove garlic, crushed

½ tsp sea salt

½ tsp ground black pepper

1 cup (240 ml) olive oil or avocado oil

For the Salad

6 cups (200 g) spring greens mix

Fresh ground black pepper and sea salt, to taste

For a Summer Salad

1 cup (150 g) blackberries

1 cup (150 g) diced melon

½ cup (55 g) slivered almonds

For a Fall Salad

1 pear, diced

¾ cup (90 g) dried cranberries

⅔ cup (70 g) chopped pecans

⅓ cup (30 g) crumbled feta cheese

For a Winter Salad

2 small tangerines, peeled into slices

⅔ cup (100 g) pomegranate arils

½ cup (55 g) slivered almonds

For a Spring Salad

⅔ cup (82 g) raspberries

⅔ cup (100 g) blueberries

1 small avocado, sliced

½ cup (75 g) pine nuts

To prepare the dressing, add the lemon zest, lemon juice, honey, Dijon mustard, red wine vinegar, garlic, salt and pepper into the blender and pulse until combined. See the note below for an optional swap for the dressing.

With the blender running, add the oil in a thin stream through the hole in the blender lid. Continue to blend until well mixed and emulsified. Thin with a little water if needed.

Arrange your salad by placing the greens in a large bowl. Toss in the fruits, nuts or cheese for your seasonal choice. Slowly add in the dressing and toss.

Serve with fresh ground pepper and sea salt to taste.

note: You can swap out lemon zest and juice in place of lime for the summertime salad. The lime pairs so well with the melon!

SMOOTHIE BOWLS 3 WAYS

Smoothie bowls are all the rage, and for good reason! Packed with veggies, fruits and protein, smoothie bowls are a healthier alternative to breakfast cereal. The best part is the many toppings that add crunch, texture and even more flavor. My kids and I love these three different versions. They're easy enough for a busy weekday morning, but also fun to enjoy on the weekends!

SERVES 2

Tropical Green Monster

½ cup (120 ml) unsweetened coconut milk

1 cup (150 g) fresh or frozen pineapple

1 banana

1 cup (15 g) loosely packed spinach leaves

1 scoop collagen protein powder, optional

Green Monster Garnish

1 kiwi, sliced

2 tbsp (15 g) shredded coconut

½ banana, sliced

1 tbsp (8 g) hemp seeds

The Chunky Monkey

½ cup (120 ml) unsweetened almond milk

1 banana

2 tbsp (30 g) almond butter or peanut butter

2 tsp (5 g) cacao or cocoa powder

2 tsp (5 g) maca powder

1 tsp cinnamon

Chunky Monkey Garnish

1 banana

2 tbsp (20 g) chopped peanuts or almonds

1 tbsp (10 g) chocolate chips

2 tsp (7 g) chia seeds

Berry Power Bowl

⅔ cup (160 ml) unsweetened almond milk

1 cup (150 g) frozen or fresh berries

½ packet of frozen dragon fruit puree, optional

1 banana

2 tbsp (20 g) chia seeds

Berry Power Bowl Garnish

½ cup (45 g) granola

½ cup (75 g) fresh berries

In a blender on low speed, blend together the milk, fruit, veggies and remaining ingredients for the smoothie bowl of your choice. After about 30 seconds, increase the blender speed to high and continue to blend until smooth and thick. You may have to pause to scrape the sides of the blender with a spatula or add additional milk.

Pour the smoothie into a bowl and garnish with toppings.

BASIL PESTO

Forget store-bought pesto. This version is so easy to make and so much tastier! Pesto is like another condiment in my house, one that I always keep on hand. We slather it over potatoes or roasted vegetables for an easy side dish, as a sauce for grilled meat and even love it on top of eggs and avocados for breakfast. Use this version for my Pesto-Stuffed Portobello Caps (page 32), or my Burrata and Tomato Pesto Zoodle Casserole (page 118).

SERVES 6

3 cups (48 g) fresh basil leaves

⅔ cup (60 g) freshly grated Parmesan cheese

⅓ cup (50 g) pine nuts or chopped walnuts

4 large cloves garlic, minced

½ tsp sea salt, plus more to taste

¼ tsp fresh ground black pepper, plus more to taste

⅔ cup (160 ml) extra virgin olive oil or avocado oil

In a high-powered blender or food processor, pulse the basil, Parmesan, pine nuts, garlic, salt and pepper. Scrape down the sides with a rubber spatula as needed.

While the motor is running, pour in the oil in a slow and steady stream. Continue to pulse until smooth. Add any additional salt and pepper to taste.

CARROT AND APPLE SALAD
WITH GINGER PEANUT DRESSING

The tangy and smooth flavors of ginger and peanut butter are a perfect accompaniment to this fabulous side salad alongside any Asian recipe! Fresh and filling on its own, I also love adding chicken to this recipe and wrapping it up in romaine lettuce for a protein-packed healthy lunch. It's great for eating on those days when I need something quick and easy! I am sure you are going to love this dressing, and you can easily double it and save half for future salads.

SERVES 2

For the Salad

2 cups (220 g) shredded carrots

2 cups (250 g) shredded Granny Smith apples

3 tbsp (18 g) diced green onion

⅓ cup (30 g) chopped almonds

¼ cup (4 g) chopped fresh cilantro

For the Dressing

¼ cup (60 g) peanut butter

2 tbsp (30 ml) tamari soy sauce or coconut aminos

2 tbsp (30 ml) apple cider vinegar

1 tbsp (15 ml) olive oil or avocado oil

1 tbsp (15 ml) sesame oil

1 tbsp (15 ml) honey

1 tbsp (15 ml) lime juice

1 tbsp (15 g) chopped fresh ginger

1 clove garlic, minced

Toss together the carrots, apples and green onion in a medium-size bowl.

In a food processor or blender, blend all the dressing ingredients: peanut butter, soy sauce, apple cider vinegar, oil, sesame oil, honey, lime juice, ginger and garlic. Blend or process until completely smooth. If the dressing is too thick, add in water by the tablespoon (15 ml).

Pour the dressing over the salad and toss to coat all the ingredients with the dressing. Serve with a topping of almonds and fresh cilantro.

AVOCADO MELON GAZPACHO

For those summer days when it's too hot to turn on the oven or stove, and you just want something refreshing and light, this gazpacho is pure gold! Slightly sweet with honeydew melon, smooth and creamy with avocado, refreshing with a combo of cucumber and mint and all topped with salty prosciutto—this soup is sure to please all!

SERVES 4 TO 6

1 large avocado, pitted and halved

1 (8-inch [20-cm]) cucumber, peeled, sliced

4 cups (950 g) cubed honeydew melon

⅓ cup (80 g) diced fennel bulb

1 jalapeño pepper with seeds removed, diced

⅓ cup (3 g) loosely packed mint leaves

¼ cup (3 g) loosely packed basil leaves

¼ cup (60 ml) fresh lemon juice

¼ cup (60 ml) white wine vinegar

½ tsp Kosher salt, plus more to taste

¼ cup (60 ml) avocado oil or olive oil

¼ cup (60 g) diced prosciutto or pancetta, for garnish, optional

Place the avocado, cucumber, melon, fennel, jalapeño, mint, basil, lemon juice, white wine vinegar and salt inside a high-powered blender.

While the motor is running, slowly add in the oil. Continue to blend for about 2 minutes until the texture is creamy and smooth. Add water by the tablespoon (15 ml) to the mixture if it's too thick.

Refrigerate until ready to serve. Salt to taste and garnish with prosciutto or pancetta.

AVOCADO CILANTRO SAUCE

I am pretty sure this will become your new favorite sauce for everything. Salads, tacos, eggs, any Mexican dish . . . so many possibilities! Avocado gives this a creamy and delicious texture and, coupled with some shelled pumpkin seeds (pepitas), the taste is out of this world! I love to keep this on hand in my fridge at all times. Be advised that it does tend to change from its original vibrant green color after a few days, but I have a feeling it won't last that long in your fridge!

SERVES 8

1 avocado

2 cloves garlic, minced

2 tbsp (30 ml) apple cider vinegar

¼ cup (40 g) pepitas

1 tsp cumin

¼ cup (60 ml) lime juice

½ cup (120 ml) water

1 tsp Kosher salt

¼ cup (8 g) fresh cilantro, chopped

½ cup (120 ml) olive oil or avocado oil

Place the avocado, garlic, vinegar, pepitas, cumin, lime juice, water, salt and cilantro into a high-powered blender or food processor. Begin to blend, and while the motor is running, slowly pour in the oil. If the sauce seems too thick, add additional water by the tablespoon (15 ml).

Store in an airtight container in the refrigerator for up to 3 days.

CHOCOLATE AVOCADO PUDDING

My family has no idea that this chocolate pudding they love and stuff their faces with has avocado as a main ingredient—I plan to keep that secret to myself! The avocado not only gives a healthy nutrient boost, it also provides a perfect thick and silky texture. This is a dessert I whip up all the time. I usually have these staple ingredients on hand, and it takes me absolutely no time to blend up this decadent dessert. It tastes best topped with some nuts, coconut shreds or even fresh fruit. You can easily halve the recipe to serve two or three people, although it is much easier to blend using the ratios below. This pudding tastes best eaten within a few days, but it probably won't last long!

SERVES 8

4 medium-size ripe avocados

½ cup (60 g) unsweetened cocoa powder

2 tsp (10 ml) vanilla extract

⅔ cup (160 ml) full-fat canned coconut milk, or coconut cream

½ tsp sea salt

¼ cup (60 ml) real maple syrup, plus more to taste

Place the avocados, cocoa powder, vanilla, coconut milk and sea salt in a food processor or high-powered blender.

While the motor is running, slowly add in the maple syrup. Stop the blender and scrape down the sides using a rubber spatula. Check to see if the pudding is sweet enough; you can add in a few more teaspoons of maple syrup to taste.

Continue to blend until all the ingredients are well incorporated, and the pudding has a fluffy or whipped texture.

Spoon the pudding into a bowl. You can serve immediately, or chill and enjoy later.

THE "DISH" ON THIS BOOK

Equipment!
The recipes are divided by the pan or appliance needed—sheet pan, skillet, Instant Pot, casserole dish, soup pot, muffin pan or blender—and consist of breakfast dishes, appetizers, soups, main courses and even simple desserts.

Blender: I am a firm believer in the best/most powerful blender—what a difference it makes when enjoying a morning smoothie or even a salad dressing! A food processor will also work in this chapter, although it may require blending in batches.

Casserole Dish: I use a 9 x 13–inch (23 x 33–cm) ceramic dish in my kitchen; I love the way it retains heat and cooks the food evenly. A less expensive glass casserole dish will also work nicely with any of the recipes. Just be sure the side rim is at least 2 inches (5 cm) tall!

Instant Pot: Likely the most hands-off kitchen device you'll ever own. I love my Instant Pot for its convenience and the fact that it cooks food 70 percent faster than any other appliance! Best used for braised meats, ethnic food and soups. I use the 7-in-1 Duo Instant Pot, but any version of the Instant Pot will work for this chapter. I use the Sauté function, Manual function and Quick Release to ensure fast cook times.

Muffin Pan: Such a great pan when you want to perfectly portion out breakfasts or sweets, but I even included a savory dinner dish (Meatloaf Muffins on page 155). I use a nonstick pan that I am always sure to grease liberally before each use.

Sheet Pan: Any 18 x 13–inch (46 x 33–cm) rectangular sheet pan with a 1-inch (2.5-cm) lip will do. Sheet pans are inexpensive, effective and perfect for a hands-off meal. They also work beautifully in allowing hot air to circulate directly around your food, giving you crispy chicken, roasted and tender meat and tasty vegetables. Recipes in this chapter range from breakfast (Potato Breakfast Nachos on page 39—yummy!) to side dishes (Roasted Cauliflower Steaks on page 43) to main courses (Greek Chicken on page 16) and desserts (delicious Healthy Oatmeal Raisin Cookies on page 47). Most main courses are complete with protein and vegetables, but you may choose to pair them with a side dish.

Skillet: The skillet is probably my favorite pan. A cast-iron or ceramic skillet that can be easily transferred to the oven is best for these recipes.

Soup Pot: A good quality stockpot or Dutch oven that can accommodate at least 5 quarts (5 L) is what I use in my kitchen. This chapter focuses solely on hearty soups and stews—my favorite!

Stock the Pantry!

The following list, while not exhaustive, provides a handy guide to the ingredients used frequently throughout the book. It's sure to set you up for success if you keep them on hand!

Coconut aminos and gluten-free tamari soy sauce: For gluten-free cooking, either of these two is a fine alternative to traditional soy sauce. Coconut aminos is free of soy but packed with amino acids and flavor. It also has significantly less sodium than dark soy sauce and can now be easily found in most grocery stores.

Flours, starches and sugars: Almond flour is my preferred choice when baking because of its nutty and buttery flavor that gives baked goods a delicious texture. It's also low carb and nutrient dense! Blanched almond flour is more fine than regular almond meal and more closely resembles white flour. I use blanched almond flour in most baked goods. Coconut flour is also used, generally for those recipes that have too much moisture. Please note: You cannot use these flours interchangeably as they each serve unique purposes in baking.

Arrowroot starch is my thickening agent of choice, acting much like corn starch. It's perfect for savory sauces and a staple in a gluten-free kitchen!

My favorite sweeteners include coconut sugar, honey or real maple syrup. These sugars are all unrefined and more pure than granulated sugar. Coconut sugar is used in most recipes as an alternative to brown sugar.

Oils and vinegars: Although most people cook with extra virgin olive oil, I much prefer avocado oil. This is from both a taste perspective (I find it lighter and more neutral tasting) and because it has a higher smoke point. However, feel free to use your favorite! Coconut oil is listed several times in the book for many of my baking recipes—I always use refined coconut oil.

I also keep my pantry stocked with red wine vinegar, apple cider vinegar and balsamic vinegar. You will almost always find some tangy element in my recipes; that vinegar ingredient is just what you need to make a meal even better.

Salt, herbs and seasonings: Pink Himalayan salt and Kosher salt are the only two salts I use in baking and cooking. Because they are both minimally processed, they have more minerals. They also pack in flavor and are lower in sodium than traditional table salt.

Spices such as cumin, smoked paprika, oregano, cinnamon, turmeric and dried basil are sprinkled throughout the book. These are kitchen staples that can be found in most grocery stores. I also use garam masala, a spice that is now commonly found in the Asian section of your grocery store.

Other pantry staples: A variety of nuts such as almonds, cashews, walnuts, peanuts and pecans are used in so many recipes. I love them for gluten-free cooking when you want added crunchy texture, or as a topping for salads and side dishes. If you have a particular nut allergy, feel free to swap out for a different nut.

Canned coconut milk is used in several sauces and Asian dishes throughout the book. My favorite brand is Thai Kitchen; I love its thickness and purity of ingredients. I do not recommend swapping out canned coconut milk in place of refrigerated coconut milk—they are not the same thing!

ACKNOWLEDGMENTS

If you're reading this, it must be true—I wrote a cookbook! First and foremost, thank you for picking up this book, reading it and hopefully cooking with it. I am glad you are trusting me with your meals!

To my handsome husband, for putting up with the craziness over the last several months. You are the best dishwasher, taste tester, honest recipe critic, grocery shopper and editor a girl could ask for. I am so glad you love my cooking and have always believed in me!

To my parents, thank you for trusting me in the kitchen at such a young age and giving me independence. From the beginning, you instilled in me a love of food and the belief that family dinners are important. Thank you for always believing in me, teaching me how to cook and for feeding me so much Mexican food as a kid!

To my sweet kiddos, Addy and Luke. Thank you for being adventurous and honest eaters. My favorite part of the day is sitting around the dinner table with both of you. I am so blessed to be your mom, and I love cooking for both of you!

To all of my official taste team: Mom and Dad Rains, Janae, Cindy, Katie, Kim, Maria, Amy, Jess and many others. Thank you for your encouragement and for making me feel like a fantastic cook. I love you all!

A special thank you to the talented Sarah Fennel. You taught me how to take gorgeous photos that bring this book to life. I am grateful for your work with this book, your expertise in creating a beautiful cover photo and chapter introductions, and for seeing my vision and running with it! You are truly brilliant.

A HUGE thank you to Page Street Publishing for bringing this book to life, designing a cookbook I am beyond excited about and for getting it out into the world!

Finally, to all of my Wholesomelicious readers and followers, thank you for all of your kind words of encouragement, and for trying so many of my recipes and helping me to make them better. You have inspired me and motivated me to continue to make the next "Best Recipe Ever." It would never be possible without all of you!

ABOUT THE AUTHOR

Born and raised in the Bay Area of California, Amy Rains has been creating recipes since her teenage years when she experimented with how to make tasty—if not always nutritious—meals on a tight budget.

Amy is the creator of wholesomelicious.com, a food blog for busy people who want to eat well. Coupling years of experience in the kitchen with her completion of an MS in Human Nutrition, Amy uses her blog to share nutrient-dense and easy-to-prepare meals with her readers.

When not in the kitchen, Amy is either teaching yoga, coaching youth baseball or softball or at the grocery store thinking about her next creation. She has traveled Europe extensively and lived in Germany for four years. Amy proudly served a combat tour in Iraq (2005–2006) while serving in the U.S. Army as an Intelligence Officer.

She now lives in Williamsburg, Virginia, with her husband, two precious kids and her adorable black Briard puppy, Tallulah.

INDEX